Does the U.S. Economy Benefit from U.S. Alliances and Forward Military Presence?

BRYAN ROONEY, GRANT JOHNSON, TOBIAS SYTSMA, MIRANDA PRIEBE

NATIONAL SECURITY RESEARCH DIVISION

For more information on this publication, visit **www.rand.org/t/RRA739-5**.

About RAND

The RAND Corporation is a research organization that develops solutions to public policy challenges to help make communities throughout the world safer and more secure, healthier and more prosperous. RAND is nonprofit, nonpartisan, and committed to the public interest. To learn more about RAND, visit www.rand.org.

Research Integrity

Our mission to help improve policy and decisionmaking through research and analysis is enabled through our core values of quality and objectivity and our unwavering commitment to the highest level of integrity and ethical behavior. To help ensure our research and analysis are rigorous, objective, and nonpartisan, we subject our research publications to a robust and exacting quality-assurance process; avoid both the appearance and reality of financial and other conflicts of interest through staff training, project screening, and a policy of mandatory disclosure; and pursue transparency in our research engagements through our commitment to the open publication of our research findings and recommendations, disclosure of the source of funding of published research, and policies to ensure intellectual independence. For more information, visit www.rand.org/about/principles.

RAND's publications do not necessarily reflect the opinions of its research clients and sponsors.

Published by the RAND Corporation, Santa Monica, Calif.
© 2022 RAND Corporation
RAND® is a registered trademark.

Library of Congress Cataloging-in-Publication Data is available for this publication.
ISBN: 978-1-9774-1004-7

Cover images: Left: Art Wager/Getty Images/iStockphoto; Right: U.S. Army photo by Staff Sgt. Micah VanDyke, 24th Press Camp/Released.

Limited Print and Electronic Distribution Rights

About This Report

The Biden administration has made strengthening alliances and partnerships a foreign policy priority, highlighting the political, military, and economic benefits the United States receives from these relationships and the associated forward military presence. However, some policymakers and analysts have called for the United States to reduce its security commitments and overseas presence, particularly in a time of fiscal constraints. In this report, we consider one element of this debate: the purported economic benefits of these security policies. This report summarizes the existing research on the economic benefits of U.S. alliances and forward military presence, highlights gaps in this research where analysts should focus future study efforts, and offers a novel analysis of the economic impact of U.S. alliances.

This report is the third in a series assessing competing claims about U.S. grand strategy. The following earlier reports in the series evaluate other dimensions of this debate:

> Bryan Rooney, Grant Johnson, and Miranda Priebe, *How Does Defense Spending Affect Economic Growth?* Santa Monica, Calif.: RAND Corporation, RR-A739-2, 2021.

> Miranda Priebe, Bryan Rooney, Caitlin McCulloch, and Zachary Burdette, *Do Alliances and Partnerships Entangle the United States in Conflict?* Santa Monica, Calif.: RAND Corporation, RR-A739-3, 2021.

This research was completed in December 2021 and conducted within the RAND Center for Analysis of U.S. Grand Strategy. The center's mission is to inform the debate about the U.S. role in the world by more clearly specifying new approaches to U.S. grand strategy, evaluating the logic of different approaches, and identifying the trade-offs each option creates. Initial funding for the center was provided by a seed grant from the Stand Together Trust. Ongoing funding comes from RAND supporters and from foundations and philanthropists.

RAND National Security Research Division

The Center for Analysis of U.S. Grand Strategy is an initiative of the International Security and Defense Policy Center of the RAND National Security Research Division (NSRD). NSRD conducts research and analysis for the Office of the Secretary of Defense, the U.S. Intelligence Community, the U.S. State Department, allied foreign governments, and foundations.

For more information on the RAND Center for Analysis of U.S. Grand Strategy, see www.rand.org/nsrd/isdp/grand-strategy or contact the center director (contact information is provided on the webpage).

Acknowledgments

The authors thank the Stand Together Trust for its support of the RAND Center for Analysis of U.S. Grand Strategy. They thank Barb Bicksler and Marco Hafner, as well as reviewers Vincenzo Bove and Angel O'Mahony, for their helpful comments on earlier drafts of this report.

Summary

Issue

In recent years, there has been a growing debate among both policymakers and analysts about the appropriate U.S. role in the world, or U.S. grand strategy. Some argue for less U.S. military engagement, meaning fewer U.S. military forces deployed abroad and a smaller number of, or more conditional, U.S. alliances. Others argue that the United States receives political, military, and economic benefits from its role as a global security purveyor. This report is the third in a series on the security and economic trade-offs associated with these competing visions for U.S. grand strategy. In this report we focus on one dimension of the decision calculus about U.S. grand strategy: the potential economic benefits of U.S. alliances and forward military presence.

Approach

We take a multistep approach to evaluating the potential impact of U.S. military engagement on the U.S. economy:

1. We identify possible pathways through which U.S. forward military presence and alliances could lead to economic benefits, drawing on theoretical work by scholars of grand strategy, political scientists, and economists.
2. We evaluate evidence from existing literature that speaks to whether economic benefits accrue through these pathways in practice.
3. We develop a model to assess how the North Atlantic Treaty Organization (NATO) alliance affects the overall level of U.S. trade and, in turn, U.S. economic welfare.

Key Findings

Despite widespread claims that there are economic benefits from U.S. alliances, we found many unanswered questions about the effects of these relationships on the U.S. economy. Our analysis led to the following key conclusions about the economic benefits of U.S. military engagement:

- U.S. alliances are associated with higher levels of trade and investment in allied countries, but scholars have not established whether alliances lead to more trade or the United States is more likely to ally with key trading partners.

- Economists have not assessed whether these higher levels of *bilateral* trade and investment translate into higher levels of *overall* U.S. trade and investment and, ultimately, economic welfare or simply divert economic activity from other, non-allied countries.
- Our new model of the relationship between alliances, bilateral trade in manufactured goods, and U.S. economic welfare suggests that the NATO alliance has been associated with higher levels of trade, which has had at least a modest positive effect on the U.S. economy.
- We are unable to assess with confidence the extent to which renegotiating or withdrawing from some existing U.S. alliances—a policy recommended by some advocates of a grand strategy of restraint—would reverse these gains and hurt the U.S. economy.
- There are examples of the United States and other powerful countries using military engagement to gain leverage in economic negotiations, but the effects of such cases on the U.S. economy are unknown.
- Foreign military conflicts impose adjustment costs on the U.S. economy, but analysts have not fully evaluated the extent to which conflicts like the war in Ukraine affect overall U.S. economic welfare.

Recommendations

Decisions about U.S. alliances and forward military presence should be based on a range of factors beyond possible economic benefits, so we do not make recommendations about whether or how the United States should change its security policies. Instead, we offer recommendations for future research that might help policymakers better understand the economic effects of alliances. We recommend that analysts pursue the following activities:

- Continue to assess whether and how military engagement increases bilateral trade and investment with U.S. allies and partners. It is unclear whether military engagement changes the behavior of partner governments, changes firm incentives, or both.
- Examine how U.S. alliances and forward presence affect U.S. economic welfare in addition to intermediate outcomes, such as bilateral trade and investment.
- Compare the economic impacts of military engagement compared with other policy options, such as free trade agreements.
- Assess the extent to which ending alliances decreases bilateral trade.
- Assess the adjustment costs that firms face as they seek new economic partners and better understand the economic effects of foreign wars on the U.S. economy.

Contents

Tables

CHAPTER 1

Introduction

The Biden administration has repeatedly highlighted the benefits the United States receives from its alliances and forward military presence.[1] Others, however, including the Trump administration and some progressive Democrats, have argued that these forms of U.S. military engagement are, in many cases, too costly.[2] Additionally, some analysts argue that U.S. security commitments and forces abroad can, counterintuitively, undermine U.S. security by exacerbating tensions with U.S. rivals.[3] As these competing claims suggest, Americans have a range of views about the effects of U.S. alliances and forward military presence. To inform this debate, the RAND Center for Analysis of U.S. Grand Strategy is analyzing the trade-offs associated with the options for U.S. military engagement—and U.S. grand strategy more broadly—in a series of reports.[4] In this report, we focus on one aspect of this broader calculation: the potential economic benefits of U.S. alliances and forward military presence.[5]

---

[1] For example, President Biden has referred to U.S. alliances as "America's greatest asset" (Joseph R. Biden, Jr., "Remarks by President Biden on America's Place in the World," The White House, February 4, 2021).

[2] Julie Hirschfeld Davis, "Trump Warns NATO Allies to Spend More on Defense, or Else," *New York Times*, July 2, 2018; Nick Wadhams and Jennifer Jacobs, "Trump Seeks Huge Premium from Allies Hosting U.S. Troops," *Bloomberg*, March 8, 2019; Uri Friedman, "The Sanders Doctrine," *The Atlantic*, February 11, 2020; Barbara Lee, "Reps. Barbara Lee and Mark Pocan Statement on House Vote for 10% Cut to Pentagon Budget," press release, Washington, D.C., July 21, 2020.

[3] See, for example, John J. Mearsheimer, "Why the Ukraine Crisis Is the West's Fault: The Liberal Delusions That Provoked Putin," *Foreign Affairs*, Vol. 93, 2014.

[4] The first report in the series considered how U.S. defense spending affects economic growth (Bryan Rooney, Grant Johnson, and Miranda Priebe, *How Does Defense Spending Affect Economic Growth?* Santa Monica, Calif.: RAND Corporation, RR-A739-2, 2021). The second report in this series asks whether U.S. alliances and partnerships entangle the United States in conflict (Miranda Priebe, Bryan Rooney, Caitlin McCulloch, and Zachary Burdette, *Do Alliances and Partnerships Entangle the United States in Conflict?* Santa Monica, Calif.: RAND Corporation, A739-3, 2021).

[5] In this report, we do not consider the related question of whether overall military strength (rather than forward presence) produces economic benefits for the United States. Commentators on both sides of this debate agree that military strength contributes to a secure homeland, economic stability, and economic growth. Where the two sides differ is in assessing the extent of military power necessary to sustain these benefits (Carla Norrlof, *America's Global Advantage: U.S. Hegemony and International Cooperation*, New York: Cambridge University Press, 2010; Daniel W. Drezner, "Military Primacy Doesn't Pay [Nearly as Much as You Think]," *International Security*, Vol. 38, No. 1, 2013, p. 54; Barry R. Posen, *Restraint: A New Founda-*

U.S. policymakers typically emphasize security, rather than economic concerns, when discussing U.S. military engagement.[6] Therefore, the size of any economic benefits gained through U.S. military engagement is likely less important to policymakers than whether such engagement deters adversaries or incentivizes allies and partners to adopt risky policies that make conflict more likely. Still, we consider some of the economic side effects of alliances for two reasons.

First, the size of the U.S. economy is one factor that determines how much the United States can afford to spend on defense, and it is therefore an important basis of U.S. military power. If the economic benefits of U.S. alliances and forward presence are substantial, then these benefits could hold security implications over time.

Second, although policymakers may not be primarily motivated by the economic effects of military engagement, the material costs of U.S. forward engagement remain a key point of contention for some policymakers and analysts. In addition to examining the costs of maintaining a forward presence, scholars must consider, as part of a comprehensive assessment, both the direct economic offsets provided by the host nation as well as the indirect economic effects. Therefore, it is worthwhile to accurately reflect what these impacts are.

Yet, the debate about U.S. grand strategy illustrates that disagreement about the economic effects of U.S. alliances and forward presence remains. *Advocates of U.S. military engagement* have generally supported the U.S. approach to the world since the end of the Cold War, including sustaining U.S. alliances and a large forward military presence in key regions. These strategists primarily focus on the security benefits of U.S. military engagement, but they also argue that U.S. alliances and forward military presence promote U.S. trade and investment and, more generally, a global economic order that disproportionately benefits the United States.[7]

The opposing school of thought, that of *restraint*, seeks to reduce the size of the U.S. military and forward military presence and to end or renegotiate some U.S. security commitments, among other changes.[8] These strategists also primarily couch their arguments in

---

tion for U.S. Grand Strategy, Ithaca, N.Y.: Cornell University Press, 2014, p. 62; Daniel W. Drezner and Nancy F. Hite-Rubin, "Does American Military Power Attract Foreign Investment?" in Jeremi Suri and Benjamin Valentino, eds., *Sustainable Security: Rethinking American National Security Strategy*, Cambridge, Mass.: The Tobin Project, 2016).

[6] For example, President Biden has stated that alliances "amplify our power as well as our ability to disrupt threats before they can reach our shores" (The White House, *Interim National Security Strategic Guidance*, Washington, D.C., March 2021).

[7] We use this term to capture a range of strategies that emphasize continued or increased U.S. military engagement abroad, such as selective engagement, deep engagement, and primacy. (For example, see Stephen G. Brooks, G. John Ikenberry, and William C. Wohlforth, "Don't Come Home, America: The Case Against Retrenchment," *International Security*, Vol. 37, No. 3, 2013; Stephen G. Brooks and William C. Wohlforth, *World Out of Balance: International Relations and the Challenge of American Primacy*, Princeton, N.J.: Princeton University Press, 2008; Hal Brands, "U.S. Grand Strategy in an Age of Nationalism: Fortress America and Its Alternatives," *Washington Quarterly*, Vol. 40, No. 1, April 2017.)

[8] For example, see Eugene Gholz, Daryl G. Press, and Harvey M. Sapolsky, "Come Home, America: The Strategy of Restraint in the Face of Temptation," *International Security*, Vol. 21, No. 4, 1997; Drezner, 2013.

security terms, but they argue that the costs of military engagement abroad outweigh the economic benefits. They also contend that the United States can sustain economic advantages even after U.S. military retrenchment, due to the size and dynamism of the U.S. economy.

Neither school in the grand strategy debate has specified the full range of these arguments theoretically or fully examined them empirically. This report, therefore, lays out the underlying logic on both sides and systematically evaluates the findings in existing empirical literature to assess whether U.S. military engagement abroad indirectly benefits the U.S. economy. In doing so, we ask the following questions:

- Does U.S. military engagement strengthen the U.S. economy by preventing war globally?
- Does U.S. military engagement promote peacetime exchange with allies and partners? If so, how do these changes affect the U.S. economy?

Key Concepts

We begin by defining our key concepts: U.S. *military engagement* and *economic benefits*. The term *military engagement* is a more expansive concept that also includes security cooperation, arms sales and subsidies, and partnerships with countries that do not have formal alliances with the United States.[9] Here we focus on the two aspects of military engagement that have been most discussed in the grand strategy debate: *alliances* and *forward military presence*.

We use the term *ally* to refer to a country with which the United States has a formal treaty obligation to come to that country's defense in the event of an armed attack. For example, this category includes Japan, South Korea, and allies within the U.S. North Atlantic Treaty Organization (NATO).[10] The term *ally* does not include U.S. partners, such as Israel and Taiwan, that have security ties with the United States but do not have a formal defense commitment from the United States.[11] Somewhat relatedly, U.S. *forward military presence* refers to the stationing of U.S. armed forces in another country outside of wartime. Although many

---

[9] Jennifer L. Erickson, "Saint or Sinner? Human Rights and U.S. Support for the Arms Trade Treaty," *Political Science Quarterly*, Vol. 130, No. 3, 2015; Carla Martinez Machain and T. Clifton Morgan, "The Effect of U.S. Troop Deployment on Host States' Foreign Policy," *Armed Forces and Society*, Vol. 39, No. 1, January 2013; Daniel Berger, William Easterly, Nathan Nunn, and Shanker Satyanath, "Commercial Imperialism? Political Influence and Trade During the Cold War," *American Economic Review*, Vol. 103, No. 2, 2013; Christopher Paul, Michael Nixon, Heather Peterson, Beth Grill, and Jessica Yeats, *The RAND Security Cooperation Prioritization and Propensity Matching Tool*, Santa Monica, Calif.: RAND Corporation, TL-112-OSD, 2013; Michael J. McNerney et al., *Assessing Security Cooperation as a Preventive Tool*, Santa Monica, Calif.: RAND Corporation, RR-350-A, 2014.

[10] U.S. Department of State, "U.S. Collective Defense Arrangements," 2017.

[11] For a discussion of the different kinds of security relationships the United States has with countries around the world, see Jennifer Kavanagh, *U.S. Security-Related Agreements in Force Since 1955: Introducing a New Database*, Santa Monica, Calif.: RAND Corporation, RR-736-AF, 2014.

U.S. allies host U.S. forces, there is not a perfect overlap between alliances and forward military presence. For example, the United States has based forces in partner countries such as Saudi Arabia, which is not a U.S. treaty ally.

In order to maintain forces abroad, and at a high state of preparedness to defend allies in the event of conflict, the United States pays *direct costs*. These costs, considered elsewhere, are not our focus here.[12] Instead, we focus on the claims that U.S. military engagement *indirectly* benefits the U.S. economy as a whole, a concept known as *economic welfare*. To measure economic welfare, economists look at national-level variables, such as economic growth or changes in the amounts of goods and services that individuals can buy (called *real purchasing power* or *inflation-adjusted wages*, also known as *real wages*).[13]

Unfortunately, as will be discussed throughout this report, scholars have not yet evaluated claims about the impact of U.S. military engagement on economic welfare. Instead, they have primarily focused on how military engagement affects two outcomes that are at least one step removed from economic welfare: changes in *bilateral trade* and *foreign direct investment (FDI)*—investments made by individuals or corporations in business enterprises in foreign countries.[14] U.S. military engagement may also result in other intermediate outcomes, such as influencing financial markets or the strength of the U.S. dollar, but there has been very little analysis in these areas.[15]

---

[12] For example, although some allies subsidize the costs of basing U.S. forces in their countries, it is generally more expensive to base forces abroad than in the United States. (See, for example, Michael Lostumbo et al., *Overseas Basing of U.S. Military Forces: An Assessment of Relative Costs and Strategic* Benefits, Santa Monica, Calif.: RAND Corporation, RR-201-OSD, 2013; Patrick Mills, Adam R. Grissom, Jennifer Kavanagh, Leila Mahnad, and Stephen M. Worman, *A Cost Analysis of the U.S. Air Force Overseas Posture: Informing Strategic Choices*, Santa Monica, Calif.: RAND Corporation, RR-150-AF, 2013.)

[13] Politicians and other analysts are sometimes interested in distributional consequences, or how groups within the U.S. economy might be affected differently by a particular policy. We return to this topic in proposing future research.

[14] FDI differs from foreign portfolio investment; FDI generally involves acquiring foreign business assets or setting up foreign business operations, while foreign portfolio investment refers to purchasing equity in foreign businesses.

[15] For example, scholars argue that major war in Asia or Europe could induce greater uncertainty that leads firms globally to behave more cautiously. Advocates of U.S. military engagement argue this may lead to reduced investment and hiring by U.S. firms and, as a result, lower U.S. economic growth. For arguments that U.S. military engagement indirectly affects the stability and strength of U.S. financial markets and the U.S. dollar, see Michael Mastanduno, "System Maker and Privilege Taker: U.S. Power and the International Political Economy," *World Politics*, Vol. 61, No. 1, 2009; Norrlof, 2010; Brooks, Ikenberry, and Wohlforth, 2013, pp. 46–48; Michael Beckley, "China's Century? Why America's Edge Will Endure," *International Security*, Vol. 36, No. 3, 2012, p. 53; Stephen G. Brooks and William C. Wohlforth, *America Abroad: The United States' Global Role in the 21st Century*, New York: Oxford University Press, 2016, p. 167; Hal Brands and Peter D. Feaver, "What Are America's Alliances Good For?" *Parameters*, Vol. 47, No. 2, Summer 2017.

Scholars have generally found increases in overall trade and investment to be associated with a country's economic growth.[16] Based on their research, however, we cannot definitively say how the U.S. economy as a whole responds to shifts in bilateral trade and FDI with allied countries.[17] This is because an increase in trade with a U.S. ally may come at the expense of trade with another country or between domestic producers and suppliers. In such cases, there may be no net effect on overall trade and FDI flows or on U.S. economic welfare. As a result, a change in bilateral trade and FDI with an ally tells us only part of the story, which represents a key limitation of the existing literature. In Chapter 5, we take a first step in addressing this disconnect by examining how changes in one of these intermediate outcomes, bilateral trade, affects economic welfare.

Competing Claims About the Economic Benefits of U.S. Forward Military Presence and Security Commitments

Advocates of U.S. military engagement argue that the United States receives economic benefits from its military engagement abroad, by preventing conflict and promoting peacetime exchange with allies and partners. Conversely, advocates of restraint argue that U.S. economic advantages can often be attributed to nonmilitary factors and that the economic benefits attributed to U.S. military engagement are overstated. Neither side in this debate has fully articulated their arguments. Therefore, as we describe the logic behind these competing claims in this section, we draw on arguments and counterarguments put forward in the larger international relations and economics literature.

Claims About U.S. Military Engagement, War, and the U.S. Economy

Advocates of U.S. military engagement argue that the foremost benefit of U.S. alliances and forward military presence derives from preventing conflict across the globe that would have a negative impact on the U.S. economy.[18] They argue that U.S. military engagement directly deters adversaries from attacking U.S. allies and partners.[19] Allies and partners are also less likely to provoke a war, these strategists contend, since U.S. military engagement reassures

---

[16] For examples from the expansive literature on these topics, see Tarlok Singh, "Does International Trade Cause Economic Growth? A Survey," *World Economy*, Vol. 33, No. 11, November 2010; Dierk Herzer, "Outward FDI and Economic Growth," *Journal of Economic Studies*, Vol. 37, No. 2, September 2010; Ross Levine and Sara Zervos, "Stock Market Development and Long-Run Growth," *World Bank Economic Review*, Vol. 10, No. 2, May 1996.

[17] These impacts are collectively referred to as "general equilibrium" effects.

[18] Robert J. Art, "A Defensible Defense: America's Grand Strategy After the Cold War," *International Security*, Vol. 15, No. 4, Spring 1991; Brooks and Wohlforth, 2016.

[19] Brands and Feaver, 2017.

them of their security and gives the United States leverage to restrain them.[20] Due to these effects on the adversary and U.S. allies and partners, this perspective holds that states with a U.S. alliance or forward military presence will be less likely to be involved in wars.

Advocates of U.S. military engagement suggest that U.S. alliances and U.S. military presence in a region also reduce the risk of interstate war more broadly, even suppressing conflicts that do not directly involve U.S. allies and partners.[21] While these strategists have not fully articulated the logic of this argument, one possible line of reasoning is that states believe a U.S. military presence indicates U.S. interest in the stability of that region and, therefore, a likelihood to intervene in wars there, inducing greater caution by all parties.[22]

Advocates of U.S. military engagement argue that preventing wars has meaningful economic benefits for the United States. In the event of war, economic disruptions do not just affect belligerent states but also regions like the United States, which are deeply involved in the global economy.[23] For example, when a U.S. trading partner is at war, its firms may be unable to maintain their prewar production levels if national resources are diverted to the conflict, production capacity is destroyed, and the movement of labor and goods is disrupted.[24] Some conflicts may also interrupt international shipping, raising transportation costs for both U.S. imports and exports.[25] Further, conflicts may have downstream economic effects, for instance, by disrupting the oil industry in driving up prices.

Advocates of U.S. military engagement note that, in addition to trade, production itself has become globalized.[26] The production of goods and services by U.S. firms relies on inputs from many other countries, and supply chains may be disrupted in the event of military conflict. Wartime disruptions would therefore force U.S. firms to search for new suppliers and export markets, hurting their production and sales as well as the U.S. economy in the

---

[20] Hal Brands, "Fools Rush Out? The Flawed Logic of Offshore Balancing," *Washington Quarterly*, Vol. 38, No. 2, 2015; Mira Rapp-Hooper, *Shields of the Republic: The Triumph and Peril of America's Alliances*, Cambridge, Mass.: Harvard University Press, 2020; Robert Kagan, "Superpowers Don't Get to Retire," *New Republic*, May 26, 2014. See also Jeremy Pressman, *Warring Friends: Alliance Restraint in International Politics*, Ithaca, N.Y.: Cornell University Press, 2011.

[21] Brooks, Ikenberry, and Wohlforth, 2013.

[22] Brooks and Wohlforth, 2016, pp. 90–92.

[23] Brooks and Wohlforth, 2016.

[24] Solomon W. Polachek and Daria Sevastianova, "Does Conflict Disrupt Growth? Evidence of the Relationship Between Political Instability and National Economic Performance," *Journal of International Trade and Economic Development*, Vol. 21, No. 3, June 2012; Alberto Abadie and Javier Gardeazabal, "The Economic Costs of Conflict: A Case Study of the Basque Country," *American Economic Review*, Vol. 93, No. 1, 2003.

[25] Conflicts need not involve U.S. trading partners to affect the U.S. economy, as even conflicts in the same region as a U.S. partner have the potential to affect the transport of U.S. imports and exports (David Hummels, "Transportation Costs and International Trade in the Second Era of Globalization," *Journal of Economic Perspectives*, Vol. 21, No. 3, Summer 2007, p. 142).

[26] Brooks and Wohlforth, 2016.

meantime. Further, the sales of U.S. multinational corporations' foreign affiliates are often much greater than domestic U.S. exports, implying this is a significant source of revenue.[27] In the event of a foreign conflict, a foreign affiliate in a war zone may see lower profits, which could result in reduced economic activity by the firm, even domestically.

Put simply, advocates of U.S. military engagement believe that economic interdependence makes the U.S. economy highly sensitive to disruptions caused by wars around the world. As a result, advocates of U.S. military engagement argue that the economic effects of foreign conflicts are substantial. These strategists argue, then, that the United States is better off paying to prevent conflict in the first place than attempting to recover economically when the conflict has begun.[28]

Conversely, advocates of restraint argue that the potential for damage to the U.S. economy caused by foreign conflicts that do not lead to direct U.S. military involvement has been overstated. Advocates of restraint acknowledge the rise of economic interdependence; however, they are skeptical that it makes the United States as vulnerable to conflict abroad as advocates of military engagement contend. Instead, they believe the U.S. economy is diverse and adaptable, allowing domestic firms, consumers, and investors to compensate for some disruptions to trade and investment. Moreover, the United States has a wide range of trading partners globally, allowing U.S. firms to find new import and export markets.[29] Finally, restrainers note that much of U.S. trade is conducted with Canada and Mexico, two states whose proximity to the United States means that the United States has an interest in their security even in the absence of an alliance or forward presence (Table 1.1).[30]

Advocates of restraint acknowledge that there would be disruptions as firms sought new partners. However, restrainers expect that these disruptions would be manageable; they contend that the United States would not be deeply affected by wartime disruptions of trade and investment, even in major markets and in locations that offer critical resources such as oil.[31] In the event of a foreign war, new markets may even arise, as the United States could increase trade and investment flows to fill the void left by belligerent states.[32] Advocates of restraint ultimately argue that the United States pays more to prevent wars than it would lose economically if those wars were to occur.

---

[27] Pol Antràs and Stephen R. Yeaple, "Multinational Firms and the Structure of International Trade," in Gita Gopinath, Elhanan Helpman, and Kenneth Rogoff, eds., *Handbook of International Economics*, Vol. 4, New York: Elsevier, 2014.

[28] Brooks and Wohlforth, 2016.

[29] Christopher Layne, *The Peace of Illusions: American Grand Strategy from 1940 to the Present*, Ithaca, N.Y.: Cornell University Press, 2007.

[30] Posen, 2014, p. 63.

[31] Layne, 2007; Posen, 2014.

[32] Eugene Gholz and Daryl G. Press, "The Effects of Wars on Neutral Countries: Why It Doesn't Pay to Preserve the Peace," *Security Studies*, Vol. 10, No. 4, 2001.

TABLE 1.1

U.S. Trade in Goods with Top Trading Partners, 2021

Country	Percentage of Total U.S. Trade	Percentage of Total U.S. Gross Domestic Product
Mexico	14.5	2.9
Canada	14.5	2.9
China	14.3	2.9
Japan	4.6	0.9
Germany	4.4	0.9
South Korea	3.5	0.7
United Kingdom	2.6	0.5
Taiwan	2.5	0.5
India	2.5	0.5
Vietnam	2.5	0.5

SOURCES: U.S. Census Bureau, 2021; U.S. Bureau of Economic Analysis, 2021.

NOTE: Data are from December 2021. Figures rounded to one decimal point.

In sum, advocates of U.S. military engagement argue that U.S. forward presence and alliances help the U.S. economy by promoting peace. For their argument to be true, we would need to find evidence of two things: that U.S. alliances and forward military presence reduce or prevent conflict, either for U.S. partners and allies or for the region as a whole; and second, that foreign conflict significantly harms the U.S. economy. If restrainers are right, we should see at most small or temporary negative effects of foreign wars on the U.S. economy. One challenge in assessing these competing claims is determining what counts as a significant impact of conflict on the U.S. economy versus a small impact. From a policy perspective, the more relevant questions these claims raise are: (1) To what extent does conflict in other regions affect the U.S. economy, even when the United States remains a non-belligerent? (2) To what extent does U.S. military engagement abroad suppress conflict?

Claims About U.S. Military Engagement and Economic Exchange in Peacetime

Another way that U.S. military engagement could theoretically benefit the U.S. economy is by boosting trade and investment in peacetime. Advocates of military engagement focus in particular on how providing security through alliances and forward presence may change partner-government behavior. Since partners value the protection that a U.S. security commitment or troop presence provides, advocates of U.S. military engagement argue that the United States might explicitly leverage these security relationships to extract more favorable terms on bilateral trade and investment agreements.[33] The United States may not even need to make this leverage explicit if partners worry that economic disagreements could disrupt their security relations with the United States, and particularly if the United States is the only viable security provider.[34] In addition, the partner nation may also offer its domestic firms direct incentives to cooperate with the United States in hopes of strengthening the alliance. Put plainly, states may willingly make economic concessions to ensure that they continue to receive U.S. security guarantees and host forward military presence.[35]

Advocates of restraint contend that, at the very least, the extent of this economic favoritism has been vastly overstated.[36] They argue that any economic concessions that have arisen could be more efficiently achieved through diplomatic negotiations or economic inducements, such as reduced tariffs, rather through military engagement.[37] Similarly, advocates of restraint argue that the threat of the United States exiting an alliance is low. Historically, they argue, the United States has been more concerned about maintaining firm alliances than its partners have.[38] As a result, security commitments do not grant the United States leverage over its allies and partners, and, in fact, the United States may be the nation granting economic concessions to maintain alliance ties.

To the extent that the United States has leverage, some advocates of restraint argue, it would only be during periods of high threat. During the Cold War, the United States and its allies were united against the threat of the Communist bloc, and the threat to U.S. partners and allies was existential. In situations like this, states may be willing to voluntarily provide concessions to the United States. However, in the more recent period, when threats have been lower, advocates of restraint argue that states have had less incentive to trade economic favors for sustaining or increasing U.S. military engagement.[39] While they have not said so

---

[33] Mastanduno, 2009; Norrlof, 2010; Brooks, Ikenberry, and Wohlforth, 2013, pp. 46–48; Beckley, 2012, p. 53; Brooks and Wohlforth, 2016, p. 167; Brands and Feaver, 2017.

[34] Joseph S. Nye, Jr., "The Changing Nature of World Power," *Political Science Quarterly*, Vol. 105, No. 2, Summer 1990; Tongfi Kim, *The Supply Side of Security: A Market Theory of Military Alliances*, Stanford, Calif.: Stanford University Press, 2016. Some countries make economic concessions as part of the alliance itself, U.S. alliance agreements do not contain such provisions (Jesse C. Johnson, "The Cost of Security: Foreign Policy Concessions and Military Alliances," *Journal of Peace Research*, Vol. 52, No. 5, 2015).

[35] Art, 1991.

[36] Drezner, 2013, pp. 62–67.

[37] Posen, 2014, pp. 61–65; Benjamin H. Friedman, Brandan Rittenhouse Green, Justin Logan, Stephen G. Brooks, G. John Ikenberry, and William C. Wohlforth, "Debating American Engagement: The Future of U.S. Grand Strategy," *International Security*, Vol. 38, No. 2, Fall 2013, p. 191. As we note, due to the lack of directly comparable research on this subject, it is difficult to adjudicate the relative effects of economic inducements and military engagement.

[38] Friedman et al., 2013, p. 191.

[39] Drezner, 2013, pp. 66–67.

explicitly, a potential implication of this logic is that the United States may get better economic terms from allies and partners in Asia as China grows more powerful.

If we find evidence that U.S. forward military presence and security commitments improve the terms of economic agreements between the United States and its partners *and* that these terms meaningfully promote U.S. growth, these findings would support the arguments made by advocates of U.S. military engagement. If, instead, we see no evidence of this bargaining leverage, if we see evidence of this leverage only with partners that face a significant threat, or if we see that beneficial trade terms have no meaningful effect on U.S. growth, these findings would support the arguments made by advocates of restraint.[40]

Beyond effects on government behavior, the international relations and economics literature suggests that U.S. military engagement may affect firm behavior. Firms respond not only to the outbreak of war but also to the risk of war. If firms *perceive* that an ally or partner faces a lower risk of conflict, they should be more willing to make long-term investments that support cross-national exchange. Transactions involving U.S. firms may be particularly attractive if it is believed that the United States will use its military to ensure the safe transit of goods between countries.

Further, when the United States has made a security commitment to a country, or when the United States keeps peacetime forces in that country, this could remove some uncertainty about the future course of the broader U.S.-partner relationship.[41] Firms have only limited information about the state of intergovernmental relationships. A public commitment such as an alliance could cause a foreign firm to believe that their nation and the United States have an alignment of interests that will sustain both security and the economic relationship between the two countries.[42] U.S. and ally firms may be more likely to engage in trade and investment because they do not fear that political or economic disputes could close markets and prevent exchange.[43]

Advocates of restraint, on the other hand, argue that the United States is an attractive economic partner first and foremost because of its large and diverse economy, not because of the military connections between states.[44] Analysts claim that firms place greater weight on the

---

[40] Advocates of military engagement argue that all alliances produce economic benefits. They do not directly engage with the question of whether U.S. bargaining leverage varies with the level of external threat the ally faces.

[41] Andrew G. Long, "Bilateral Trade in the Shadow of Armed Conflict," *International Studies Quarterly*, Vol. 52, No. 1, 2008; Andrew G. Long and Brett Ashley Leeds, "Trading for Security: Military Alliances and Economic Agreements," *Journal of Peace Research*, Vol. 43, No. 4, 2006; Garett Jones and Tim Kane, "U.S. Troops and Foreign Economic Growth," *Defence and Peace Economics*, Vol. 23, No. 3, 2012.

[42] Edward D. Mansfield and Rachel Bronson, "Alliances, Preferential Trading Arrangements, and International Trade," *American Political Science Review*, Vol. 91, No. 1, 1997; Benjamin E. Bagozzi and Steven T. Landis, "The Stabilizing Effects of International Politics on Bilateral Trade Flows," *Foreign Policy Analysis*, Vol. 11, No. 2, April 2015.

[43] Certain alliances are designed specifically to provide dispute-resolution mechanisms (Long and Leeds, 2006).

[44] Gholz, Press, and Sapolsky, 1997, pp. 44–45.

political institutions and policy choices of a potential economic partner than on the security relationship between the two states.[45] The United States has an institutional system based in the rule of law and a long-standing position of support for free trade, increasing foreign firms' confidence in doing business with U.S. corporations. For these scholars, security relationships are of much less concern; therefore, the presence of a U.S. alliance or military forces in another country should have little effect on the level of economic exchange.

Report Organization

In the chapters that follow, we turn to the empirical evidence from existing literature that underlies the competing claims of U.S. military engagement advocates and advocates of restraint. For each competing claim identified, we evaluate both quantitative and qualitative evidence from the economics and political science literature. In doing so, we evaluate the methodological strengths and weaknesses of key studies in this literature and assess the extent to which these studies speak to the current circumstances in the United States.

In Chapter 2, we examine the connection between U.S. military engagement, foreign wars, and the U.S. economy. First, we examine how foreign wars would affect the U.S. economy by examining historical cases of U.S. non-belligerence in wars and broader economic trends for non-belligerent states during wartime. We then examine whether U.S. military engagement helps prevent conflict, thereby avoiding these economic costs.

In Chapter 3, we look at bilateral trade and investment flows to examine the claim that U.S. military engagement results in increased economic activity between the United States and its partners and allies.

In Chapter 4, we seek to better understand the mechanism by which these increases occur. We consider the effects of U.S. military engagement on U.S. bargaining leverage in economic negotiations and on firm behavior.

In Chapter 5, we develop a model that shows how U.S. military engagement affects trade and, in turn, U.S. economic welfare. Specifically, we employ a common model that demonstrates the impact of alliances on bilateral trade so that we can explore the effects of alliances on overall U.S. trade and economic welfare. We use this model to consider how changes in trade patterns due to shifts in NATO alliances would affect consumer purchasing power—the ratio of wages to average consumer prices—in the United States.

We conclude, in Chapter 6, with a description of what the literature can and cannot tell us about the effects of U.S. military engagement on the U.S. economy, and we recommend research areas that still need to be explored in order to inform debates about the economic consequences of U.S. grand strategy.

---

[45] Drezner and Hite-Rubin, 2016.

CHAPTER 2

Does U.S. Military Engagement Strengthen the U.S. Economy by Preventing Conflict Globally?

In this section, we explore the relationship between U.S. military engagement, war, and the U.S. economy, evaluating each piece of the logic chain individually. First, we examine the impact of foreign conflicts on the U.S. economy. Second, we examine the role of U.S. alliances and forward military presence in preventing conflict.

Foreign Military Conflicts Disrupt U.S. Trade and Investment, but It Is Unclear How Much This Affects Economic Growth

In March 2022, exploring the impact of foreign conflicts on the U.S. economy is especially timely and vital.[1] As the Russian invasion of Ukraine progresses, analysts have noted how supply chains have been disrupted, resulting in shortages of key production materials.[2] Energy prices have risen dramatically, affecting both global shipping and consumers.[3] The economic impacts have been magnified as corporations work to comply with sweeping economic sanctions on Russia.[4] Some analysts have already predicted that the economic effects on the United States will be significant, with rising oil prices, historic inflation rates, and market disruptions likely to lead to slower U.S. economic growth.[5] At the same time, corporations have been preparing since before the war to mitigate the economic impacts of the

---

[1] Jeanna Smialek and Ana Swanson, "What Does Russia's Invasion of Ukraine Mean for the U.S. Economy?" *New York Times*, February 23, 2022.

[2] Ana Swanson, "Ukrainian Invasion Adds to Chaos for Global Supply Chains," *New York Times*, March 1, 2022.

[3] Abha Bhattarai, Tony Romm, and Rachel Siegel, "U.S. Economy Appeared Ready to Surge, but Russia's Invasion of Ukraine Could Send Shockwaves," *Washington Post*, February 25, 2022.

[4] Patricia Cohen, "Within Days, Russia's War on Ukraine Squeezes the Global Economy," *New York Times*, March 1, 2022.

[5] Matt Egan, "Why the Russian Invasion Will Have Huge Economic Consequences for American Families," *CNN*, February 24, 2022.

invasion.[6] Therefore, the overall effect on the U.S. economy—and the global economy—will likely not be known for quite some time. We can, however, examine how foreign wars have historically affected the U.S. economy.

Participants in the grand strategy debate disagree about how foreign wars would affect the U.S. economy if the United States remained non-belligerent. Studying this question is challenging for a number of reasons. First, while the economic costs of war to belligerents have been well studied,[7] there has been less analysis on the costs to non-belligerents, which is our focus here. Second, there have not been many cases of major military conflicts with periods of U.S. non-belligerence since World War I; so, few analysts have considered the U.S. experience in depth. Third, even where such cases existed, forming baseline expectations of how the U.S. economy would have evolved in the event that conflict had not occurred is difficult. Finally, the global economy is constantly changing. The impact of conflict on non-belligerent economies may shift over time, particularly in an increasingly globalized world, making it hard to know how well past experience would apply to future conflicts. We explain here how existing studies have dealt with these challenges, what they have found, and how much confidence we can have in extrapolating from their findings.

Economic Growth

Only one study attempts to link foreign war with both an intermediate economic outcome, specifically trade, as well as with overall U.S. economic growth.[8] In the study, Gholz and Press examine the period prior to U.S. entry into World War I (July 1914–April 1917).[9] The authors find that the outbreak of war resulted in temporary disruption to U.S. trade, with both belligerents and other non-belligerents, due to increases in shipping rates, uncertainty about exchange rates, and changing demands in belligerent countries, among other factors. However, U.S. exports recovered and significantly surpassed prewar levels in 1915 and 1916. This recovery occurred, in part, because the United States replaced some belligerents as suppliers to non-belligerents in Europe, South America, and Asia. Germany's announcement of unrestricted submarine warfare hurt U.S. trade in 1917, but the authors were unable to assess whether trade would have recovered had the United States not entered the war in April.[10]

---

[6] Mark Maurer, "U.S. Companies Say They Are Monitoring Impact of Russia-Ukraine Crisis," *Wall Street Journal*, February 24, 2022.

[7] See, for example, Steven J. Yamarik, Noel D. Johnson, and Ryan A. Compton, "War! What Is It Good For? A Deep Determinants Analysis of the Cost of Interstate Conflict," *Peace Economics, Peace Science and Public Policy*, Vol. 16, No. 1, 2010; Solomon W. Polachek and Daria Sevastianova, "Does Conflict Disrupt Growth? Evidence of the Relationship Between Political Instability and National Economic Performance," *Journal of International Trade & Economic Development*, Vol. 21, No. 3, 2012; Vally Koubi, "War and Economic Performance," *Journal of Peace Research*, Vol. 42, No. 1, 2005.

[8] Gholz and Press, 2001.

[9] The paper also briefly considers the effects of the Iran-Iraq war on the U.S. economy.

[10] Gholz and Press, 2001, pp. 26–28.

Gholz and Press make a rough estimate of how changes in trade and other economic exchanges during the war affected overall U.S. economic growth. They note that the United States faced a recession both before and after the war and was both a non-belligerent and a belligerent in the conflict, complicating any interpretation of changes in U.S. economic growth in this period. Still, they contend that three facts provide important insights about the effects of war on a non-belligerent United States. First, the U.S. economy was larger after the war than before, despite the postwar recession. Second, the long-term trend of growth that had taken place prior to the war generally resumed after the postwar recession.[11] In other words, in Gholz and Press's view, the United States stayed on the same long-term growth trajectory in spite of the economic costs of war that occurred during years that it was non-belligerent. Finally, the authors found that U.S. wealth increased during its period as a non-belligerent, because overseas profits increased more than the costs of adjustment for U.S. businesses, although there is great uncertainty around their estimate.[12] Viewed from this perspective, Gholz and Press contend that the United States suffered only temporary and, in the long term, minimal economic costs due to the war.

However, this analysis has important limitations. First, the authors' baseline of U.S. economic growth in the absence of war is not very precise and is also open to dispute. The authors use the average growth rate seen between 1900 and 1925, but this average trend masks significant year-to-year variation. For example, GNP declined between 1907 and 1908 and grew at a much higher rate than average in 1923. Importantly, the U.S. economy had experienced a recession in 1913 and early 1914, before the outbreak of the war and after experiencing an upward economic trajectory. These fluctuations make it difficult to separate the effects of the war from a typical cycle of recession and recovery. Second, it is difficult to conclude how much weight to put on these results from the short period in which the United States was a non-belligerent, which is further complicated by subsequent involvement in the conflict. As a result, it is perhaps best to treat this as an example that is consistent with, but does not conclusively prove, the argument that the U.S. economy can adjust and recover from disruptions caused by foreign wars.

Given that the literature on how war affects economic growth in non-belligerent countries is limited, we also examine the impact of war on non-belligerent parties for two intermediate economic outcomes: bilateral trade and investment.

Bilateral Trade

The evidence suggests that, *on average*, bilateral trade decreases significantly between war participants and non-belligerent states. In the most prominent study on this topic, Glick and

---

[11] Gholz and Press, 2001, p. 36.

[12] Gholz and Press, 2001, p. 40.

Taylor examine the short- and long-term impacts of war on trade.[13] The authors examine a substantial time period, 1870 to 1997, comparing levels of trade between pairs of states during peacetime, wartime, and postwar periods.[14] They find that trade between belligerents and non-belligerents declines 5 to 12 percent, on average, during wartime and that the effects persist for up to seven years following conflict termination. They further find that the major wars—World War I and World War II—had the most dramatic effects.[15] Other scholars have highlighted deviations from this average trend. Gholz and Press show that U.S. trade increased during its period of non-belligerence in World War I, and Gowa and Hicks similarly find that trade between the Central Powers and non-belligerent states rose because prewar suppliers for the Central Powers were now in enemy countries.[16] Thus, these average trends do not apply in all cases.

Looking for greater nuance in the relationship, Feldman and Sadeh, covering the period of 1885 to 2000, considered whether export flows between belligerent and non-belligerent states depend on the national interests and security commitments of the non-belligerent party.[17] The authors use the similarity of alliance commitments between a non-belligerent and belligerent state as a proxy for the similarity in the two states' national interests. The authors find that when a non-belligerent state has shared alliances with one side of a conflict, its exports to the opposing side decrease by nearly the same extent as between the warring parties themselves. This result suggests that a war involving current U.S. allies may result in decreases in trade between the United States and war participants, even if it remains a non-belligerent.

Trade can also be interrupted by conflict in the same geographical area. In a study examining trade from 1948 to 2006, Qureshi finds that trade between two non-belligerent states decreases by roughly 5 percent when one of the non-belligerent states shares a border with

---

[13] Examining both short- and long-term impacts is potentially important, as scholars have argued that war could destroy obsolescent infrastructure and increase the motivation to rebuild, leading to long-term improvements in the nation's economy. (See Abramo F. K. Organski and Jacek Kugler, "The Costs of Major Wars: The Phoenix Factor," *American Political Science Review*, Vol. 71, No. 4, 1977.)

[14] This statistical technique is known as Ordinary Least Squares with fixed effects. This approach holds constant any characteristics between the pairs of states—even those that are difficult to observe or quantify—that do not shift over time. This means that we have greater confidence that any changes in trade can be more accurately attributed to the presence or absence of war in these different time periods (Reuven Glick and Alan M. Taylor, "Collateral Damage: Trade Disruption and the Economic Impact of War," *Review of Economics and Statistics*, Vol. 92, No. 1, February 2010; Long, 2008).

[15] Glick and Taylor, 2010. The authors also use a two-stage analysis—first predicting the likelihood of war and then using those predictions as a substitute for war onset—and find that their results do not significantly change, indicating that it is unlikely that the causal arrow runs in the opposite direction, with changes in trade driving conflict.

[16] Joanne Gowa and Raymond Hicks, "Commerce and Conflict: New Data About the Great War," *British Journal of Political Science*, Vol. 47, No. 3, 2017.

[17] Nizan Feldman and Tal Sadeh, "War and Third-Party Trade," *Journal of Conflict Resolution*, Vol. 62, No. 1, 2018.

a state engaged in internal or international conflict.[18] She finds that bilateral trade does not rebound for roughly five years following conflict and that this result is robust to several different model specifications and sources of data.[19] Bilateral trade may therefore decrease for the United States if conflict occurs on the border of a key trading partner. These results suggest that a war in Poland, for example, may impact U.S. trade not only with Poland but also with Germany.

Multiple studies have found that the effect of war on trade with belligerents is different for imports to and exports from the belligerent.[20] This difference occurs because conflict that takes place in the exporting country destroys assets that support production. As a result, U.S. imports may be more affected by foreign wars than are U.S. exports. This distinction may be particularly important given that the United States is a net importer.

However, recent work has argued that these deleterious effects of conflict on bilateral trade may be decreasing due to globalization. As Sadeh and Feldman argue, globalization allows states to substitute trade partners or replace trade with forms of FDI.[21] The authors find that as their measures of globalization—global FDI, financial openness, and World Trade Organization (WTO) membership—increase, the negative effects of militarized disputes on bilateral trade between belligerent and non-belligerent states dissipate. The authors use a fixed effects technique in which they isolate trends in both trade over time with the same partner and trade in the same year with all partners, allowing them to more cleanly identify changes that occur due to increasing globalization.[22] This analysis provides suggestive evidence that the modern economy may overcome some of the deleterious effects of conflict on trade for non-belligerent states.

In summary, there is evidence that foreign wars can affect the economy of non-belligerent parties by suppressing trade, as belligerent and non-belligerent trade decreases following conflict onset. However, this finding has to be applied cautiously to the contemporary

---

[18] Mahvash Saeed Qureshi, "Trade and Thy Neighbor's War," *Journal of Development Economics*, Vol. 105, 2013.

[19] Further, Qureshi demonstrates that the results are robust to an analysis in which she first predicts the likelihood of conflict in a neighboring state by using the average number of military personnel on active duty (as a percentage of total population) in all neighboring countries, which should be otherwise unrelated to bilateral trade between any particular pair of states.

[20] Long, 2008; Valentina Marano, Alvaro Cuervo-Cazurra, and Chuck C. Y. Kwok, "The Impact of Conflict Types and Location on Trade," *International Trade Journal*, Vol. 27, No. 3, June 2013. The authors examine the effects of both interstate and intrastate conflict. Philippe Martin, Thierry Mayer, and Mathias Thoenig, "Make Trade, Not War?" *Review of Economic Studies*, Vol. 75, No. 3, July 2008.

[21] Tal Sadeh and Nizan Feldman, "Globalization and Wartime Trade," *Cooperation and Conflict*, Vol. 55, No. 2, January 6, 2020.

[22] They also consider the possibility that their results may be driven by states choosing to engage in conflicts in ways that are less damaging economically. They find no evidence of states opting for different approaches to conflict, though they cannot rule this possibility out. Specifically, as globalization increases, they find that the negative effects of conflict disappear for the target rather than for the initiator of the dispute.

United States for several reasons. First, as discussed in Chapter 1, the importance of this finding for the U.S. economy is not straightforward, because the literature focuses on *bilateral* trade between belligerents and non-belligerents rather than on *overall* trade by non-belligerents. Second, this finding is an average effect for all non-belligerents. Given the size of the U.S. economy and its role in the global economy, the United States may differ from the average non-belligerent state. More analysis is needed to determine exactly how states with large and diverse economies do or do not deviate from this general pattern.

Third, the evidence also shows that these effects are conditional. As we noted, U.S. imports are more likely to be affected by foreign wars than by exports. Further, because the evidence suggests that the location of the conflict and the belligerents involved are important, it is likely that only some conflicts—for instance, a conflict in Europe featuring a NATO partner—are likely to affect U.S. trade.

Finally, the evidence suggests that the overall impact may decrease over time. In a globalized economy, U.S. businesses can find new trade partners to mitigate the effects of these disruptions. There are certainly some costs associated with these changes; however, little has been done to assess the costs of redirecting trade during a conflict, making it difficult to assess how disruptions to trade resulting from conflict ultimately affect economic growth.

Investment

In addition to altering trade patterns, conflict may also suppress U.S. FDI. Outward FDI can improve U.S. economic growth by allowing firms to produce finished goods at lower costs and by allowing the United States to import cheaper inputs from foreign countries. In comparison to the literature on the impact of interstate conflict on trade, the literature on the impact of interstate conflict on FDI is less developed. This literature also examines a shorter and more recent time frame, meaning that many studies cover periods when there have not been any major great power wars of the sort that scholars of grand strategy are primarily concerned with.

One study by Bussmann does examine interstate conflict's effect on FDI flows and FDI stock—the total level of direct investment within a country at a given point in time.[23] This study finds that countries involved in a fatal conflict see a decrease in FDI stock and FDI inflows as a percentage of GDP.[24] In addition, Bussmann finds evidence that there is a significant decrease in the FDI stock in belligerent states, which persists even three years after the dispute. The results suggest that U.S. firms may need to alter previously productive

---

[23] Formally, FDI stock is the value of capital and reserves (within a country and within a given year) that is attributable to multinational corporations based in other countries, plus the net value of debt owed by foreign affiliates to their parent organizations.

[24] Margit Bussmann, "Foreign Direct Investment and Militarized International Conflict," *Journal of Peace Research*, Vol. 47, No. 2, 2010. In the baseline model, in which Bussmann does not consider endogeneity, she finds no significant effect for FDI stock. Bussmann uses two different methodologies in which she first predicts the onset of fatal conflict and then predicts its impact on FDI stock; in each, the effect is significant.

investments in the event of a conflict in a host nation, either by changing investment patterns or reducing foreign investment entirely. Related research by Busse and Hefker supports the finding that interstate war suppresses inward FDI and that internal conflict does as well.[25]

In the extreme, conflict may disrupt U.S. foreign investment by forcing firms to exit the market. Indeed, the empirical research supports this argument.[26] Dai, Eden, and Beamish provide evidence on the relationship between conflict and firm exit by examining both intra- and interstate wars.[27] They examine over 1,000 Japanese multinational enterprise subsidiaries active in 20 countries that experienced conflict between 1987 and 2006, and they find that subsidiaries that are closer to conflict zones are significantly more likely to exit the market. Further, the exit rate is higher for more valuable subsidiaries.[28] If U.S. firms operate similarly, this finding suggests that U.S. firms located near a conflict zone may, in some cases, need to pay the costs of moving their enterprises to another location or reduce production entirely.[29]

Overall, the evidence suggests that multinational corporations reduce FDI to belligerent states and may be forced to withdraw capital or exit the foreign market altogether. However, both the breadth and depth of this research is limited. Further research is needed to understand which industries are affected, how long it takes firms to transition from investment in one foreign nation to another, and how costly this transition is. Without this information, it is difficult to assess how changes in investment flows would affect the United States in particular.

Summary

Ideally, we would have information about how foreign wars affect the U.S. economy in particular. However, this type of research is not available. Therefore, we draw on the broader literature regarding how war affects non-belligerent states' trade with and investment in belligerent countries. The evidence from this literature suggests that, on average, foreign conflicts do

---

[25] Matthias Busse and Carsten Hefeker, "Political Risk, Institutions and Foreign Direct Investment," *European Journal of Political Economy*, Vol. 23, No. 2, 2007.

[26] Li Dai, Lorraine Eden, and Paul W. Beamish, "Caught in the Crossfire: Dimensions of Vulnerability and Foreign Multinationals' Exit from War-Afflicted Countries," *Strategic Management Journal*, Vol. 38, No. 7, 2017, pp. 1478–1498.

[27] These results are supported by studies in the literature that examine only civil conflict. Adriana Camacho and Catherine Rodriguez, "Firm Exit and Armed Conflict in Colombia," *Journal of Conflict Resolution*, Vol. 57, No. 1, 2013, pp. 89–116.

[28] The "value" of a multinational enterprise subsidiary is based on its strategic location and its size relative to other subsidiaries owned by the multinational enterprise.

[29] There is also some evidence that a history of war is a determinant of where multinational firms choose to invest. Barry uses firm-level data to explicitly model the initial decision to invest in a country for multinational corporations. Barry finds that the entry of new firms is positively associated with the amount of time that has passed since the state's last domestic conflict, both for severe civil conflicts and for lower-level disputes. Colin M. Barry, "Peace and Conflict at Different Stages of the FDI Lifecycle," *Review of International Political Economy*, Vol. 25, No. 2, 2018.

hurt trade between belligerent and non-belligerent states, though there are exceptions. The effects of wars on non-belligerents depends on the context, with wars that involve U.S. allies or that take place near key trading partners potentially being the most disruptive. In addition, there is evidence to support the claim that non-belligerent investment is also disrupted, although this evidence includes fewer studies.

As a result, we conclude that many foreign conflicts will impose at least some adjustment costs on the U.S. economy; indeed, both sides in the grand strategy debate acknowledge this. Where they disagree is on how deep and long-lasting these effects will be. The existing literature does not provide enough information for us to assess how quickly firms can adapt in today's world.[30] More research must therefore be done to understand how impactful these adjustment costs will be for the U.S. economy and, ultimately, how they affect U.S. economic growth.

U.S. Alliances, on Average, Reduce the Risk of Conflict, but the Effect of Forward Presence Is More Complex

Given that there is some evidence that the United States and its partners suffer economic costs from foreign wars, we now ask whether U.S. alliances and a U.S. forward presence decrease the likelihood of such conflicts. In particular, we ask the following: (1) Does a U.S. military presence reduce the likelihood of war by making war less likely for U.S. allies and partners in particular? (2) Does a U.S. military presence reduce the likelihood of war by increasing regional stability?

Again, there is limited literature on the U.S. experience specifically; therefore, we draw from the extensive literature on the effects of alliances on conflict globally. This literature considers war and conflicts short of war, collectively known as *militarized interstate disputes*. Militarized interstate disputes include everything from the threat of military violence to the outbreak of war. Examining this broad class of disputes allows us to understand how alliances prevent interstate competition from reaching the threshold of militarization. Although preventing war is most consequential, lower-level conflicts can make cooperation more difficult, fuel arms racing, and make a future war more likely.[31]

For the questions of interest here, we care about whether U.S. military engagement makes states less likely to be involved in conflict. The literature on these topics often provides a more granular examination, asking whether states are more likely to initiate conflict or be targeted

---

[30] For example, Gholz and Press, 2001, use an estimate from Lichtenberg that does not directly examine adjustment costs due to war and, at thirty years old, may be out of date (Frank R. Lichtenberg, "Estimation of the Internal Adjustment Costs Model Using Longitudinal Establishment Data," *Review of Economics and Statistics*, Vol. 70, No. 3, 1988).

[31] See Michael P. Colaresi and William R. Thompson, "Hot Spots or Hot Hands? Serial Crisis Behavior, Escalating Risks, and Rivalry," *Journal of Politics*, Vol. 64, No. 4, November 2002; Paul D. Senese and John A. Vasquez, *The Steps to War: An Empirical Study*, Princeton, N.J.: Princeton University Press, 2008.

by others. For our purposes, these distinctions do not matter, so we consider what is known about both outcomes and, ultimately, how alliances and forward presence affect allies' and partners' conflict involvement, when taken as a whole.

Are states in alliances less likely to be involved in conflict? We focus here on defensive alliances, alliances that commit a state to provide military support only in the event of an attack on its ally—the only type of alliance in which the United States is involved. Scholars have consistently found that, on average, states in defensive alliances are less likely to be involved in conflict.[32] These findings have been strengthened more recently as scholars have taken steps to address some of the methodological challenges to studying the relationship between alliances and conflict. The most pressing of these challenges is the impact of selection effects, or the possibility that states with allies may be systematically different from those without allies—a factor that might affect the initial choice of whether to form an alliance. To avoid misleading results, scholars have to account for the possibility that the decision to form an alliance is driven by the likelihood of conflict.

When scholars have used matching techniques—a common quantitative method for accounting for potential selection effects—they have found similar results, which strengthens our confidence in the findings. Matching analyzes the conflict propensity for pairs of states that differ in terms of whether an alliance is present but that, otherwise, have similar characteristics known to affect the likelihood of conflict.[33] Matching allows us to consider only observable characteristics of states that analysts choose to match on, such as level of democracy or economic size. Where important drivers of conflict are not included in the matching process, however—because they are difficult to quantify or are not considered, for example—selection effects may persist. Matching is therefore not a perfect method; however, the consistency of the results when using this method does lend credence to the idea that alliances make interstate conflict less likely.

In addition, these findings hold regardless of whether we examine conflict initiated by or against the ally. In a previous report, we described the literature that finds that states with defensive alliances are less likely to initiate conflict.[34] Scholars have also repeatedly

---

[32] Brett Ashley Leeds, "Do Alliances Deter Aggression? The Influence of Military Alliances on the Initiation of Militarized Interstate Disputes," *American Journal of Political Science*, Vol. 47, No. 3, 2003; Jesse C. Johnson and Brett Ashley Leeds, "Defense Pacts: A Prescription for Peace?" *Foreign Policy Analysis*, Vol. 7, No. 1, 2011; Brett Ashley Leeds and Jesse C. Johnson, "Theory, Data, and Deterrence: A Response to Kenwick, Vasquez, and Powers," *Journal of Politics*, Vol. 79, No. 1, 2017; Brett V. Benson, "Unpacking Alliances: Deterrent and Compellent Alliances and Their Relationship with Conflict, 1816–2000," *Journal of Politics*, Vol. 73, No. 4, October 2011; Thorin M. Wright and Toby J. Rider, "Disputed Territory, Defensive Alliances and Conflict Initiation," *Conflict Management and Peace Science*, Vol. 31, No. 2, 2014.

[33] Leeds and Johnson, 2017.

[34] Priebe et al., 2021b.

found that states in defensive alliances are much less likely to be the target of a military dispute.[35]

These average effects could disguise some variation within alliances. It is therefore important to consider the extent to which these findings reflect the dynamics in current U.S. alliances. One major way in which the United States differs from other partners is in terms of military power. Looking at all states that have defensive alliances, Johnson, Leeds, and Wu examine the role of ally capabilities in deterring adversaries.[36] Their measure takes two forms—the combined military capabilities of all of a state's defensive allies and the combined military capabilities of the state's strongest single alliance, which may be bilateral or multilateral. They find that states with stronger allies are less likely to be targeted with a militarized interstate dispute. These results suggest that the United States should, by virtue of its military capabilities, be better able to deter its ally's adversaries and to reduce the likelihood of conflict. Further, our previous report found that the best available evidence suggests that states that depend more on the military power of their alliance partners are less likely to initiate conflict.[37]

Furhmann and Sechser measure another aspect of U.S. alliances and military power—the nuclear umbrella.[38] They find that defensive alliances with a nuclear power deter adversaries from initiating a militarized dispute, whereas those with nonnuclear powers have no significant effect on disputes. Since few states possess nuclear weapons, this finding must in no small part result from the deterrent impact of the United States. We note that since the authors do not control for the conventional capabilities of a state's nuclear allies, we cannot be sure whether conventional capabilities, rather than having a nuclear ally, may explain their findings. The United States, for example, can defend allies through conventional and nonconventional means and the authors do not consider the relative deterrent power of these different forms of military might. Yet in either instance, the United States would be expected to deter adversaries strongly.

---

[35] Leeds, 2003; Johnson and Leeds, 2011; Leeds and Johnson, 2017; Wright and Rider, 2014. Counterevidence provided by Kenwick et al. found that allies were more likely to be targeted by an adversary following alliance formation in the 1816–1945 time frame, though their methods have been called into question by Morrow. Morrow also presents descriptive evidence that certain pairs of states may be more likely to become involved in a conflict following alliance formation, but he does not explore this evidence in a fully specified model. (Michael R. Kenwick, John A. Vasquez, and Matthew A. Powers, "Do Alliances Really Deter?" *Journal of Politics*, Vol. 77, No. 4, 2015; James D. Morrow, "When Do Defensive Alliances Provoke Rather Than Deter?" *Journal of Politics*, Vol. 79, No. 1, 2017.)

[36] Jesse C. Johnson, Brett Ashley Leeds, and Ahra Wu, "Capability, Credibility, and Extended General Deterrence," *International Interactions*, Vol. 41, No. 2, 2015.

[37] Priebe et al., 2021b. See Songying Fang, Jesse C. Johnson, and Brett Ashley Leeds, "To Concede or to Resist? The Restraining Effect of Military Alliances," *International Organization*, Vol. 68, No. 4, 2014.

[38] Matthew Fuhrmann and Todd S. Sechser, "Signaling Alliance Commitments: Hand-Tying and Sunk Costs in Extended Nuclear Deterrence," *American Journal of Political Science*, Vol. 58, No. 4, 2014.

Studies by Bak and Clare suggest that alliances have a lesser impact on the likelihood of conflict when the ally is farther away, as the United States is from most of its allies.[39] Both studies find that defensive alliances have a strong deterrent effect when states share a border. Bak finds that a state that is more distant from its allies is more likely to be targeted by an adversary than a state with proximate allies. Bak also finds that while the military strength of the ally is important in deterring challenges from adversaries, the deterrent impact of these military capabilities diminishes as geographic distance increases. However, it is not clear if either study can be applied to a state like the United States that has a large number of forces deployed in and near key allied countries.[40] Further, Bak also finds that these effects are dissipating over time, meaning that factors such as advanced technology and capabilities could be decreasing the importance of physical distance.

Within alliances, relationships also play an important role in conflict involvement.[41] Johnson, Leeds, and Wu find greater deterrent effects when an alliance stipulates higher levels of peacetime coordination, such as integrated military commands, foreign military presence, or basing access.[42] These represent effects on average, but the results should apply to the United States due to its defensive alliances, substantial military capabilities, and high levels of peacetime coordination with allies. The sum total of the evidence suggests that the trends for defensive alliances more generally should strongly apply to U.S. alliances.

U.S. allies. RAND researchers have found that the significance of results depends on how a question is modeled statistically. Previous RAND research has examined the relationship between conflict and alliance with the United States and found that U.S. allies are less likely to be involved in interstate war and more likely to be involved in disputes short of war, all things being equal.[43] However, the authors of the current study primarily seek to analyze the effect of a U.S. forward presence, not U.S. alliances. Since U.S. allies often host U.S. forces, the researchers include alliances as a control to separate the effects of the two types of military engagement.

---

[39] Daehee Bak, "Alliance Proximity and Effectiveness of Extended Deterrence," *International Interactions*, Vol. 44, No. 1, May 2017; Joe Clare, "The Deterrent Value of Democratic Allies," *International Studies Quarterly*, Vol. 57, No. 3, 2013.

[40] Bak controls for the deployment of U.S. forces as a robustness check and finds his core relationship holds, but he notes that he does not investigate the conditioning effect of forward presence on alliances.

[41] Clare also examines the relevance of the ally in the democratic state's alliance and trade portfolios, but he does not adjust for the democracy's military or economic power, making the results difficult to interpret. Clare, 2013.

[42] Johnson, Leeds, and Wu, 2015. The authors do not consider the selection of alliances, but given that the sample contains only states with alliances, this likely does not bias their results.

[43] Angela O'Mahony, Miranda Priebe, Bryan Frederick, Jennifer Kavanagh, Matthew Lan, Trevor Johnston, Thomas S. Szayna, Jakub P. Hlavka, Stephen Watts, and Matthew Povlock, *U.S. Presence and the Incidence of Conflict*, Santa Monica, Calif.: RAND Corporation, RR-1906-A, 2018; Bryan Frederick, Stephen Watts, Abby Doll, Ashley L. Rhoades, and Meagan L. Smith, *Understanding the Deterrent Impact of U.S. Overseas Forces*, Santa Monica, Calif.: RAND Corporation, RR-2533-A, 2020.

This technique is appropriate for examining the impact of troop deployments. However, it makes it difficult to assess the impact of U.S. alliances. Because the measures are closely tied, it is difficult statistically to assess the role of alliances distinct from the forces that often follow these agreements.[44] More recent work that also examines alliances and troop deployments has supported the finding that U.S. alliances reduce the likelihood of interstate war, but it has found no evidence that U.S. alliances increase the likelihood of disputes short of war.[45] Further, this work explicitly models the selection process for U.S. military engagement, increasing our confidence in the direction of the relationship.

Countries that host U.S. forces. The effects of U.S. military deployments on host nations engaging in international conflict have been explored to a much lesser extent in the existing literature.[46] Martinez Machain and Morgan find some evidence that U.S. military presence makes host countries less likely to be targets of a high-intensity military disputes, including war.[47] Given that this analysis looks at U.S. military presence and disputes in the same year, we cannot determine the direction of causality. However, if anything, examining U.S. military presence and disputes in the same year should decrease the likelihood of finding the result the authors uncover, since U.S. forces would seem more likely to increase rather than decrease in response to conflict. Since the authors do not control for other forms of U.S. military engagement, such as the presence of a U.S. alliance, it is difficult to say for certain that troop deployments, as opposed to the more broadly construed "military engagement," reduce conflict. However, this finding does support the broader relationship between U.S. military engagement and conflict reduction.

Previous RAND research has considered this question in greater depth. Researchers have found that states hosting U.S. forces are, on average, more likely to be targets of conflicts initiated by U.S. adversaries.[48] Frederick et al. expands this analysis and finds that these effects differ by the type of U.S. forces. More mobile forces are associated with more disputes

---

[44] This effect is what happens when models control for what are called intervening variables, which in this case can be thought of as one mechanism through which the independent variable leads to changes in the dependent variable.

[45] Stephen Watts, Bryan Rooney, Gene Germanovich, Bruce McClintock, Stephanie Pezard, Clint Reach, and Melissa Shostak, *Deterrence and Escalation in Competition with Russia: Executive Summary*, Santa Monica, Calif.: RAND Corporation, RR-A720-2, 2022.

[46] In two excellent works, Braithwaite and Kucik find significant evidence that U.S. troop deployments reduce the likelihood of civil conflict, while Azam and Thelen find that U.S. troop deployments increase the likelihood of terrorist violence in oil-producing countries and reduce the likelihood elsewhere. (Alex Braithwaite and Jeffrey Kucik, "Does the Presence of Foreign Troops Affect Stability in the Host Country?" *Foreign Policy Analysis*, Vol. 14, No. 4, 2018; Jean-Paul Azam and Véronique Thelen, "Foreign Aid Versus Military Intervention in the War on Terror," *Journal of Conflict Resolution*, Vol. 54, No. 2, 2010.)

[47] Martinez Machain and Morgan, 2013. In several other robustness checks, this effect is not significant. However, the fixed effects model is the most defensible methodologically. We do note that the analysis does not control for many of the factors that may cause both troop deployments and affect conflict, though it is difficult to assess how much this biases the results.

[48] O'Mahony et al., 2018b; Frederick et al., 2020; Watts et al., 2022.

initiated against U.S. host countries, while heavier forces, including armored, mechanized, artillery, and combat aviation units, are associated with decreases in higher-level conflict but increases in lower-level conflict such as threats or displays of force.[49] The authors argue that it is possible either that light forces may be threatening because of their mobility or, alternatively, that all troop deployments are threatening but that only heavy forces also have a deterrent effect. These differences should be further explored moving forward. These findings are robust to analyses in which the authors explicitly model selection effects, which may be an issue as the United States might choose to locate its forces in areas where conflict is more likely.[50]

These results provide little direct evidence that U.S. forces deter attacks on U.S. partners. It is possible that these forces serve as a greater threat to potential adversaries than the deterrent value they would provide. However, it is important to clarify that, while a U.S. military presence is associated with an increased likelihood of a partner being targeted with a conflict short of war, the authors do not find evidence that this effect extends to war. Still, it cannot be ruled out that conflict will not escalate to full-scale war, in part, due to a U.S. presence.

RAND research has also examined the question of whether U.S. forces embolden partners to initiate militarized disputes.[51] This analysis has shown that an in-country U.S. military presence is associated with a decreased likelihood that the U.S. partner will initiate lower-intensity conflict, and it shows no significant impact on the likelihood that the U.S. partner will initiate high-intensity conflict. Consistent with the results for alliances, there is little evidence that partners are emboldened by a U.S. military presence.

Regional stability. A key argument made by advocates of U.S. military engagement is that U.S. security commitments and a forward U.S. military presence promote regional stability. The effect of U.S. alliances on conflicts in nearby states has not been examined systematically. However, previous RAND research has examined the effect of a U.S. forward military presence on nearby conflict.

---

[49] While heavy U.S. ground forces appear to deter high-intensity conflict against the partner, it does not have the same effect on low-intensity conflict, as the probability of low-intensity conflict actually increases in the presence of heavy U.S. ground forces. Further, light ground forces appear to have escalatory effects for low- and high-intensity conflict. Only U.S. air defense artillery within the partner nation shows no escalatory effects, although it also decreases the likelihood of only low-intensity conflict.

[50] The authors first calculate the likelihood of U.S. forces being deployed to a particular partner based on its likelihood of conflict, and then use this to weight observations in the data to account for this selection effect. This weighting technique is called inverse propensity score weighting. In practice, observations in the treatment group (those states that receive U.S. forces) are weighted by the inverse of their propensity (their likelihood of receiving a U.S. military presence, as determined by the initial empirical model), while those in the control group (those that do not receive U.S. forces) are weighted by the inverse of the complement of this propensity. Frederick et al., 2020, pp. 152–155. See also David A. Freedman and Richard A. Berk, "Weighting Regressions by Propensity Scores," *Evaluation Review*, Vol. 32, No. 4, 2008, pp. 392–409.

[51] Angela O'Mahony et al., *U.S. Presence and the Incidence of Conflict*, Santa Monica, Calif.: RAND Corporation, 2018a.

This research has found that a U.S. forward presence is associated with a lower likelihood of war and high-intensity conflict in the region surrounding the state in which they are located.[52] This finding applies to both the likelihood that a nearby state will be targeted in a higher-level conflict and the likelihood that it will initiate a conflict. However, the same is not true for lower-level conflict. The empirical analysis suggests that a U.S. presence in the region is associated with a lower likelihood of initiation of both high- and low-level conflict by U.S. treaty allies.[53] However, non-U.S. allies located in the same region as countries with a U.S. military presence have a higher likelihood of initiating low-intensity conflict, although the overall risk of conflict remains low. One interpretation is that U.S. military presence does not suppress disputes, but it does limit the level that states are willing to escalate to in order to resolve disputes. Further research could clarify the nature of this relationship.

Summary

Strong evidence suggests that, on average, states in alliances are less likely to be involved in conflict. Given the conditions under which researchers have found this relationship to be the strongest and given suggestive evidence from studies that focus on the United States, this finding likely applies to the U.S. case specifically. However, it is difficult to pin down an exact magnitude for this effect.

The effect of U.S. forward presence on conflict is more conditional. Researchers have found that U.S. forward presence is associated with less war and high-intensity conflict in the region in which they are located. The effect on the host nation is not consistent across studies and differs by the type of U.S. forces, with more mobile forces being associated with an increase in conflict and heavier forces being associated with a decrease in conflict. Thus, the effect of U.S. forward presence on conflict appears to hinge on which forces are deployed and where they are located.

---

[52] O'Mahony et al., 2018b; Frederick et al., 2020; Watts et al., 2022. Frederick et al. find that, similar to the host nation effects, these effects differ by the type of U.S. forces.

[53] O'Mahony et al., 2018b.

CHAPTER 3

Does U.S. Military Engagement Increase Bilateral Trade and Investment in Peacetime?

Our findings suggest that U.S. military engagement can prevent some economic disruptions that would occur if its allies and partners became embroiled in conflict. It remains to be seen, however, whether U.S. military engagement can also induce greater economic activity during *peacetime*. In this section, we consider the relationship between U.S. military engagement and two of our intermediate outcomes—U.S. security partners' trade with and investment in the United States—that may improve U.S. economic welfare.

Globally, Alliances Are Associated with Increased Trade, and the Evidence Suggests This Should Also Be True for U.S. Alliances in Particular

We begin by examining the link between U.S. military engagement and trade. The strongest empirical evidence linking U.S. military engagement and economic benefits examines global alliances.[1] Scholars have consistently found that states trade more with their allies than with other states.[2] Although this literature generally does not focus specifically on U.S. alliances, there is reason to believe that the findings apply to the United States.

First, much of this literature focuses on trade by major powers rather than by all states globally.[3] While it is difficult to compare the United States with other nations, major powers belong to a class of states that have greater economic and military capabilities and thus represent cases that are most comparable with the United States. Second, evidence suggests that

---

[1] For early examples, see Joanne Gowa and Edward D. Mansfield, "Power Politics and International Trade," *American Political Science Review*, Vol. 87, No. 2, 1993; James D. Morrow, Randolph M. Siverson, and Tressa E. Tabares, "The Political Determinants of International Trade: The Major Powers, 1907–90," *American Political Science Review*, Vol. 92, No. 3, September 1998.

[2] Scholars have also found that alliances reduce trade volatility (Bagozzi and Landis, 2015).

[3] Andrew G. Long, "Defense Pacts and International Trade," *Journal of Peace Research*, Vol. 40, No. 5, 2003; Joanne Gowa and Edward D. Mansfield, "Alliances, Imperfect Markets, and Major-Power Trade," *International Organization*, Vol. 58, No. 4, 2004.

the defensive alliance—the type of alliance held by the United States—is the type that leads to increased trade between partners, as opposed to other forms of alliances.[4]

Third, while most research on this topic considers relationships between pairs of states, there is reason to believe that there are greater network effects of alliances on shaping international trade.[5] Researchers have found that states at the center of large alliance networks experience the largest increases in trade. Further, states are more likely to trade not only with their allies but also with partners of those allies.[6] This suggests that dyadic measures of trade may understate some of the benefits of alliances. Given the expansive U.S. security commitment network, this would imply larger benefits for the United States.

Additional variations in the relationship between alliances and trade has been identified that suggests the relationship may be stronger today. In the sample of major powers and their trading partners, the association between alliances and trade is stronger in the post–World War II era.[7] These findings could suggest either that the relationship between alliances and trade is growing as globalization increases or, alternatively, is stronger during periods of bipolarity.[8] These studies have not yet been extended into the post–Cold War time frame when the distribution of power became unipolar, which would more definitively answer this question.

A previous RAND study examines the relationship between security agreements and trade specifically for the United States.[9] Egel et al. find that an increase in the number of security agreements a state has with the United States corresponds to higher levels of bilateral trade overall and especially U.S. imports.[10] The authors argue that this means that states with a closer security relationship with the United States also have higher levels of trade. The

---

[4] Long, 2003.

[5] Matthew O. Jackson and Stephen Nei, "Networks of Military Alliances, Wars, and International Trade," *Proceedings of the National Academy of Sciences*, Vol. 112, No. 50, 2015.

[6] Dotan A. Haim, "Alliance Networks and Trade: The Effect of Indirect Political Alliances on Bilateral Trade Flows," *Journal of Peace Research*, Vol. 53, No. 3, 2016. Further, this effect does not appear to be driven by a specific alliance community, and it holds even though alliance communities shift over time.

[7] Gowa and Mansfield, 2004. In addition, exports in industries with increasing returns to scale show increases to a greater extent than those with constant returns to scale.

[8] Morrow et al. also find suggestive, but not significant, evidence that the results are stronger during bipolarity and, in fact, find a negative relationship between alliances and trade pre–World War II. However, the authors do not include measures such as fixed effects that would provide greater confidence in their results. James D. Morrow, Randolph M. Siverson, and Tressa E. Tabares, "The Political Determinants of International Trade: The Major Powers, 1907–90," *American Political Science Review*, Vol. 92, No. 3, September 1998.

[9] Daniel Egel, Adam R. Grissom, John P. Godges, Jennifer Kavanagh, and Howard J. Shatz, *Estimating the Value of Overseas Security Commitments*, Santa Monica, Calif.: RAND Corporation, RR-518-AF, 2016. The effect for imports is roughly twice the size as the effect for U.S. exports.

[10] The authors treat disparate treaty types as equal; for example, they combine alliance commitments with neutrality pacts and agreements on principles as nonproliferation. Using data provided by the authors, we find that the existence of any single security commitment remains a strong predictor of bilateral trade. However, these results are also sensitive to the removal of a small number of observations.

authors consider the size and growth rate of the U.S. economy to account for the possibility that U.S. economic power, rather than its security relationships, is associated with higher levels of trade.[11]

These results are, however, not robust. When the authors restrict their sample to only those states in which the United States conducts *any* form of trade, a restriction that has been used by others in this literature, the estimated relationship is no longer statistically significant. This change in the population of cases drops just 1.3 percent of observations in their sample, and yet the authors get different results. Since the results prove sensitive to such a small change in the sample, we assert that more research is needed before concluding that U.S. security agreements, including alliances, are associated with more trade.

Egel et al. also use their analysis of the relationship between bilateral trade and U.S. security agreements to estimate the effect of a 50 percent reduction in global U.S. treaties on the U.S. economy.[12] The authors estimate that a 50 percent reduction in security agreements would cause U.S. GDP to fall by as much as $490 billion, about 2 percent of the U.S. GDP in 2021. This focus on economic welfare is a useful advancement over most of the literature, which considers only intermediate outcomes like trade. The model requires a number of assumptions, most notably the assumption that for every dollar in U.S. bilateral trade that is lost as a result of the removal of security commitments, 85 cents would be deducted from U.S. GDP and 15 cents would be retained through redirection to other productive uses.[13] Since their analysis does not directly consider the way that other parts of U.S. or global economy might adjust, their finding may be an overestimate of the effects of ending security commitments on the U.S. economy. In Chapter 5, we present a model that addresses some of these limitations.

Scholars analyzing the effect of security agreements on trade in the United States thus come to conclusions that are similar to those of studies that examine a larger number of countries—alliances are associated with higher levels of bilateral trade—but with lower confidence in the results. It is not clear, however, that alliances cause trade to increase. Some scholars have argued that states form alliances to protect their existing trading partners and that, therefore, trade affects alliance choices rather than the reverse. Several studies have considered this possibility, known as reverse causality, by examining the role of trade in predicting alliance formation. These scholars have found no significant results from their analyses.[14] In other words, they find no evidence that trade levels explain alliance formation.

However, at least one study has argued that states form alliances to protect economic interests. Fordham finds that in the post-1950 time period, levels of trade between a major power such as the United States and a minor power increase the probability of alliance

---

[11] The authors also find evidence of spillover effects. The association between U.S. security commitments and U.S. imports with other states in the region is also positive and significant.

[12] Egel et al., 2016.

[13] Egel et al., 2016, p. 68.

[14] Mansfield and Bronson, 1997; Gowa and Mansfield, 2004.

formation.[15] Using the author's replication files, we find the results are much stronger for the United States than for other major powers.[16]

Given this conflicting evidence, the exact direction of this relationship remains in question and the topic warrants further research. Scholars on both sides of the debate have investigated the possibility of reverse causation, but they have found conflicting evidence. Scholars arguing that alliances cause higher levels of trade have found no significant effect of trade on alliance formation, while scholars arguing that alliances are formed to protect trade relationships have found no significant effect of alliance formation on trade. Given that these scholars examine disparate samples and time frames and use different modeling techniques, it is difficult to diagnose the reason for these divergent findings or assess which result is most applicable to the U.S. case.

The most likely result, perhaps, is that trade increases the probability of alliance formation *and* alliances increase the flow of trade. In other words, even if economic relationships contribute to alliance formation, alliances may still influence trade. This possibility would be consistent with another finding: alliances magnify the effect of economic agreements.[17] Mansfield and Bronson find that allies that are also part of the same preferential trading arrangement engage in markedly greater trade than those who are not allies.[18] This conclusion suggests that alliances and economic agreements could be complementary, not substitutes, although more research is needed to explore this possibility.

In addition to looking at levels of bilateral trade, some research has examined the impact of alliances on the probability of two states forming a bilateral trade agreement.[19] Eichengreen, Mehl, and Chitu examine economic agreements in which states granted mutual tariff concessions or granted "most favored nation" status in the period prior to World War I.[20] The authors find that defense pacts are associated with a higher probability of states forming an economic agreement by as much as 21 percentage points and that these results are robust to a number of different specifications. Of particular note, the authors use a matching technique

---

[15] Benjamin O. Fordham, "Trade and Asymmetric Alliances," *Journal of Peace Research*, Vol. 47, No. 6, 2010.

[16] Following a similar logic, Poast finds that, in the sample of European states from 1860 to 1945, offers of trade linkages made military alliance negotiations more likely to succeed and result in an agreement. Paul Poast, "Does Issue Linkage Work? Evidence from European Alliance Negotiations, 1860 to 1945," *International Organization*, 2012.

[17] Long and Leeds find that trade among allies that have provisions for economic cooperation written into their alliance agreements is higher than trade among non-allied states and among allied states that have no formal provisions for economic cooperation; however, they examine only the pre–World War II time frame. Long and Leeds, 2006.

[18] Mansfield and Bronson, 1997.

[19] For evidence of the impact of bilateral investment treaties on investment, see Peter Egger and Michael Pfaffermayr, "The Impact of Bilateral Investment Treaties on Foreign Direct Investment," *Journal of Comparative Economics*, Vol. 32, No. 4, 2004; Eric Neumayer and Laura Spess, "Do Bilateral Investment Treaties Increase Foreign Direct Investment to Developing Countries?" *World Development*, Vol. 33, No. 10, 2005.

[20] Barry Eichengreen, Arnaud Mehl, and Livia Chiţu, "Mars or Mercury Redux: The Geopolitics of Bilateral Trade Agreements," *The World Economy*, Vol. 44, No. 1, 2021. The data come from Robert Pahre, *Politics and Trade Cooperation in the Nineteenth Century*, New York: Cambridge University Press, 2008.

to compare cases in which an alliance has been formed with similar cases in which an alliance has not been formed. Their findings remain the same when they use this technique, giving us greater confidence that alliances lead to more agreements and not the other way around.[21] These results suggest that even if the strong U.S. economy is attractive to outside economic partners, as advocates of restraint argue, U.S. alliances can enhance these effects.

Going beyond the presence of an alliance, more limited evidence suggests an association between U.S. trade and U.S. forward military presence.[22] Egel et al. find that U.S. forward presence is associated with increased trade with host nations.[23] They find this effect both strong and significant for U.S. imports at the bilateral level, though it is not statistically significant for U.S. exports.[24] Since they do not control for the presence of a U.S. alliance when testing the effect of troop deployments on trade, troop deployments might function as a proxy for U.S. alliances in the statistical analysis. When we use their data to include alliances and U.S. military personnel in the same model, the size and significance of the effect of personnel decreases, while the effect of security commitments remains substantively and statistically significant.[25] This result suggests that we can have greater confidence that alliances have an impact on trade than do U.S. military personnel.

Biglaiser and DeRouen find evidence that a larger U.S. military force corresponds to increased trade between the United States and developing partners while accounting for the presence of a U.S. alliance commitment.[26] The authors also find evidence that U.S. forces increase when trade increases, supporting the idea that the relationship goes both ways.

In sum, evidence suggests that alliances are associated with higher levels of trade. The literature has not settled the important question of whether alliances lead to higher levels of trade or vice versa. The literature has also not considered the possibility that both outcomes are true—that alliances may be formed, in part, to protect trading relations and that alliances further increase bilateral trade once they are formed. The scholarly literature finds more limited evidence that there is a positive association between U.S. military presence and trade with host nations. Given these findings, there does appear to be a positive association between U.S. military engagement and bilateral trade. However, beyond

---

[21] Along similar lines, Martin, Mayer, and Theonig find that the presence of a military alliance is associated with an increased likelihood of joint participation in a regional trade agreement. Philippe Martin, Thierry Mayer, and Mathias Thoenig, "The Geography of Conflicts and Regional Trade Agreements," *American Economic Journal: Macroeconomics*, Vol. 4, No. 4, 2012.

[22] There is also evidence that host nations benefit economically. Uk Heo and Min Ye, "U.S. Military Deployment and Host-Nation Economic Growth," *Armed Forces & Society*, Vol. 45, No. 2, 2019; Jones and Kane, 2012.

[23] Egel et al., 2016. These effects hold for all personnel, when excluding all states with whom the United States has zero trade and are otherwise significant for a U.S. Air Force or U.S. Army presence.

[24] As before, the authors find evidence of spillover effects. There is a significant and positive effect of U.S. troop presence on U.S. imports at the regional level.

[25] Specifically, the effect of personnel is significant only at the 0.10 level.

[26] Glen Biglaiser and Karl DeRouen, Jr., "The Interdependence of U.S. Troop Deployments and Trade in the Developing World," *Foreign Policy Analysis*, Vol. 5, No. 3, 2009.

debates about whether military engagement causes increases in trade, the literature does not capture our true variable of interest—U.S. economic welfare. In other words, based on the existing literature, we cannot exclude the possibility that higher levels of bilateral trade with allies simply divert trade from other partners and have a neutral or even negative effect on the U.S. economy as a whole.

There Is Suggestive but Inconclusive Evidence That Investment Is Higher Between the United States and Its Security Partners

The impact of military engagement on investment has received less attention in the literature. The evidence that does exist suggests that defensive alliances of the type possessed by the United States are associated with a larger flow of FDI between certain types of states.[27] Specifically, alliances are associated with increased FDI flows between high-income states and low-income states, with no significant effect between pairs of high-income states. For example, these results suggest that the increase in FDI from the United States to Romania in recent years may have, in part, resulted from Romania's entry into NATO in 2004. However, if Finland, a significantly richer country, were to join NATO, there may not be an analogous increased FDI from the United States to Finland.[28] The authors use country-pair fixed effects to capture aspects of the relationship between countries that do not change over time and to reduce concerns about omitted variables influencing their findings. The authors' methodology does raise some concerns about selection effects, as the authors do not explicitly account for the possibility that states choose their alliance partners partly for economic reasons. This means, we cannot be sure of the extent to which alliances cause more FDI versus the other way around.

Much like trade agreements, alliances are associated with the formation of bilateral investment treaties (BITs), which privileges the investment relations between the two states.[29]

---

[27] Quan Li and Tatiana Vashchilko, "Dyadic Military Conflict, Security Alliances, and Bilateral FDI Flows," *Journal of International Business Studies*, Vol. 41, No. 5, 2010.

[28] For data on FDI flows between the United States and Romania, see Bureau of Economic Analysis, "Direct Investment by Country and Industry," webpage, July 22, 2021.

[29] Elkins, Guzman, and Simmons's seminal study on BITs was not focused on alliance questions, so alliances were only a control variable rather than the key independent variable in the model. Therefore, the model was designed to control for confounding variables for their relationship of interest—in this case, the relationship between market competition and the probability of signing a BIT—and thus the authors did not explicitly account for omitted variable bias for the relationship between bilateral investment treaties and security commitments. However, more recent work focused on alliances has found evidence supporting this result (Zachary Elkins, Andrew T. Guzman, and Beth A. Simmons, "Competing for Capital: The Diffusion of Bilateral Investment Treaties, 1960–2000," *International Organization*, Vol. 60, No. 4, 2006; Zhiyuan Wang and Hyunjin Youn, "Locating the External Source of Enforceability: Alliances, Bilateral Investment Treaties, and Foreign Direct Investment," *Social Science Quarterly*, Vol. 99, No. 1, May 10, 2017).

In addition, scholars have found that the presence of an alliance is associated with an increase in the likelihood that BITs, once agreed upon, will be ratified domestically.[30] Most notably, the presence of an alliance and a bilateral investment treaty together is associated with an even greater increase in FDI.[31] Wang and Youn examine this relationship for 30 FDI source countries and 105 FDI host countries; the United States is present in the data as both a source country and a host country. The authors find that while the effect of a BIT alone on bilateral stocks of FDI is significant, when two states share a security alliance, the effect of a BIT is substantially greater.[32]

Biglaiser and DeRouen examine the relationship between U.S. forward presence and U.S. investment.[33] To account for differences in the pool of states selected for U.S. investment and those not selected, the authors first investigate the probability that U.S. firms will choose to invest in a given country and then, given that choice, investigate the level of investment. They find evidence that the likelihood of FDI from the United States into developing countries increases with its military presence.[34] They also find that the level of U.S. investment increases in states that host U.S. forces. This research does not fully adjudicate the mechanism by which FDI shifts. In other words, it may be due to U.S., allied, or host nation policy or to the risk assessment of firms. Moreover, none of this research takes the next step to assess the net impact of these increases in FDI on the U.S. economy.

The existing literature suggests that alliances are associated with an increase in the level of FDI between developed and developing countries. It also suggests that alliances make economic agreements more likely and magnify their effects. There is limited evidence of the effects of U.S. military presence on FDI, however, which inhibits our ability to draw a definite conclusion. Overall, more analysis is needed to examine the extent to which economic relationships cause higher levels of military engagement versus the other way around. However, the consistency of the effects suggests that U.S. engagement likely affects economic activity.

---

[30] Yoram Z. Haftel and Alexander Thompson, "Delayed Ratification: The Domestic Fate of Bilateral Investment Treaties," *International Organization*, Vol. 67, No. 2, April 2013.

[31] Wang and Youn, 2017.

[32] In their baseline specification, Wang and Youn find that the effect of a ratified BIT alone on bilateral stocks of FDI is, in fact, very large, roughly doubling bilateral FDI when compared with states that do not share a BIT. When two states share a security alliance, the effect of a ratified BIT is substantially greater— roughly three times the size of the effect of a BIT in the absence of an alliance. This pattern holds across specifications, although the authors note that magnitudes decrease under more rigorous robustness checks, including fixed effects. The authors do not discuss the differences in magnitude.

[33] Glen Biglaiser and Karl DeRouen, Jr., "Following the Flag: Troop Deployment and U.S. Foreign Direct Investment," *International Studies Quarterly*, Vol. 51, No. 4, 2007.

[34] In addition, the authors control for the Cold War and post–Cold War time frame and find that the effects are still significant.

It Is Unclear Whether U.S. Military Engagement Increases a Security Partner's Economic Activity with the United States

We find evidence that trade and investment between the United States and its partners increases when there is greater U.S. military engagement. This might happen for one of two reasons. First, U.S. military engagement might increase the economic productivity of the partner nation by promoting stability. Several studies have found an association between U.S. forward presence and host nation economic development.[35] Alternatively, partner nation governments or firms could redirect economic exchange toward the United States. This distinction could be thought of as the difference between the United States receiving the same share of an increasing economic pie or receiving a larger share of it. The U.S. economy could potentially benefit from either type of economic shift, but distinguishing between the two gives us better insight into the relationship between U.S. military engagement, trade, and investment.

To understand this question, we need to examine not the volume of economic activity overall, but its composition. We find only a single study that does so. Bove et al. examine this question for U.S. deployments and trade. They find that increases in U.S. forward presence positively affect the share of a host nation's trade that is with the United States, with a roughly 1 percent increase in the U.S. share of trade following a 10 percent increase in U.S. forward presence.[36] They further find that this relationship is most robust for U.S. exports, regardless of industry.[37] In addition, the authors explicitly address the direction of causality by first performing an analysis in which they predict U.S. troop deployments using data on host nation military spending per soldier.[38] The intuition behind this analysis is that host nation military spending per soldier is negatively related to U.S. deployments, because they are substitutes, but host nation military spending per soldier is otherwise unrelated to bilateral trade and therefore not subject to the same concerns about the direction of causality as U.S. deployments.[39]

On the whole, there is a dearth of evidence that distinguishes between an increase in the volume of economic activity between the United States and its partners and a redirection of economic activity to the United States. Further, none of these studies examine the role of security commitments.[40] This remains a significant gap in the literature.

---

[35] Jones and Kane, 2012, pp. 225–249; Tim Kane, "Development and U.S. Troop Deployments," *Foreign Policy Analysis*, Vol. 8, No. 3, 2012, pp. 255–273; Heo and Ye, 2019, pp. 234–267.

[36] Vincenzo Bove, Leandro Elia, and Petros G. Sekeris, "U.S. Security Strategy and the Gains from Bilateral Trade," *Review of International Economics*, Vol. 22, No. 5, 2014.

[37] The authors also find the effect holds for overall U.S. imports and for imports in certain categories, such as fuels and food and beverage.

[38] The authors do so through an instrumental variable analysis.

[39] While host nation military spending might reflect the anticipation of conflict, host nation spending *per soldier* is more likely to be driven by domestic political and economic factors.

[40] This, in part, motivates our decision to look at the impact of U.S. alliances more closely in Chapter 5.

Summary

The evidence discussed in this chapter supports the viewpoint that U.S. military engagement is associated with a higher volume of economic activity between the United States and its partners. There is significant evidence of a positive relationship between military engagement and bilateral trade, particularly for U.S. alliances. There is also evidence of a positive relationship between military engagement and bilateral investment, though there are fewer studies on the topic. There is reason to believe that the literature's broader findings apply to the case of the United States. We note, however, that the direction of the relationship should be further explored, as alliances may be used to protect important economic partners and improve economic relations between states. Further, studies should examine whether the share of U.S. trade and investment increases in addition to the volume.

What is less clear is the mechanism by which these changes occur, as an increase in bilateral trade could result from changes in government behavior, firm behavior, or both. Further, it is not immediately clear how these bilateral changes in trade and investment translate into the overall effect of U.S. military engagement on U.S. economic welfare. We focus on these questions in the following two chapters.

CHAPTER 4

Why Might U.S. Military Engagement Increase Bilateral Trade and Investment?

The previous chapter examined changes in bilateral trade and investment between the United States and its partners as a result of military engagement. In this chapter, we will explore possible reasons for this association. There are multiple pathways by which U.S. military engagement could increase the level of economic activity between the United States and its partners. We constrain our focus to two potential pathways. First, we examine evidence of partner government behavior changing directly as the result of U.S. military engagement, through the exertion of bargaining leverage. Second, we consider theoretical explanations for how U.S. military engagement might change firm behavior and discuss why current research does not provide sufficient analysis to explore this pathway.

The United States Has, at Times, Gained Leverage in Economic Negotiations due to Military Engagement

The first way that U.S. military engagement might increase trade and investment between the United States and its allies is by changing the behavior of partner governments. While there are multiple possible explanations for the behavior of partner governments, advocates of U.S. military engagement most prominently argue that such engagement leads partner nations to grant the United States more favorable terms in economic agreements.[1] To examine this pathway quantitatively, we would ideally examine the impacts that security commitments and U.S. forward presence have on the terms of trade between states, or on barriers to such trade, such as tariffs. However, the empirical literature has not looked at these questions.[2] Even the most exemplary study cited above, by Bove et al., accounts for the existence

---

[1] For example, Gowa and Mansfield and Long suggest that governments redirect trade to gain the benefit of a security externality, as both states grow in economic power. Long, 2003; Gowa and Mansfield, 1993.

[2] Berger et al. find that, following CIA interventions to install or support leaders in foreign nations, these states shifted the balance of their foreign trade toward the United States and away from foreign countries. Since this occurred primarily in economic areas in which U.S. businesses had a comparative economic disadvantage and most frequently through direct government procurement, the authors argue that this resulted from increased U.S. political influence. This is, however, a more extreme exertion of military engagement than we consider here. Berger et al., 2013.

of a free trade agreement but does not account for its terms; neither does it seek to examine how the agreement was reached.[3]

Evidence of the bargaining leverage pathway is therefore largely qualitative and focuses on the leverage offered by security commitments in state-to-state negotiations. Mastanduno argues that the United States was granted outsized economic support by its partners during the Cold War time frame, even without making explicit links to its security commitments.[4] For example, Mastanduno notes that West Germany feared the possibility that U.S. economic woes could force the United States to reevaluate its forward presence. This conclusion was further highlighted when the Johnson administration did, in fact, remove a division from West Germany in 1967. As a result, West Germany was willing to revalue its currency and reduce trade protection to ensure the level of U.S. economic power that was required by its ongoing security provision.

Stokes and Waterman, in addition to Mastanduno, argue that the United States used its security leverage to achieve Japanese economic adjustment in the 1980s.[5] The United States, in response to a growing trade imbalance with Japan as well as to the appreciation of the dollar, began putting pressure on Japan to open Japanese markets to U.S. trade and investment. This resulted in a number of negotiations between the two nations, including the market-oriented sector-selective talks, which had modest success in reducing barriers to trade, and the Plaza Accord, which reduced the value of the dollar relative to the yen. State Department documents suggest both that the United States was more willing to take retaliatory measures in the realm of defense at this time and that the Japanese government expressed concern that defense pressures would increase in light of trade demands. Stokes and Waterman therefore argue that it was only when Japan began to perceive that U.S. defense commitments were dependent on Japanese economic adjustment that it became willing to undertake these economic measures.[6]

The evidence provided in this case relies on U.S. policymaker beliefs and therefore requires direct confirmation of this position from the perspective of the Japanese government. More explicit discussion of the security benefits of economic agreements has been found in recent years. Kim notes that when talking about the proposed Trans-Pacific Partnership, Japanese Prime Minister Abe argued that it would go "far beyond just economic benefits. It is also about our security. Long-term, its strategic value is awesome."[7]

Advocates of restraint argue that during the Cold War, the United States and its allies were united against the threat of the Communist bloc and that allies were willing to voluntarily

---

[3] Bove, Elia, and Sekeris, 2014.

[4] Mastanduno, 2009, pp. 132–136. Mastanduno questions the extent to which these benefits will remain in the post–Cold War era, pp. 149–150.

[5] Doug Stokes and Kit Waterman, "Security Leverage, Structural Power and U.S. Strategy in East Asia," *International Affairs*, Vol. 93, No. 5, 2017, pp. 1047–1049. Mastanduno, 2009, pp. 140–141.

[6] Stokes and Waterman, 2017, pp. 1047–1049.

[7] Kim, 2016. The United States pulled out of the Trans-Pacific Partnership negotiations in 2017.

provide concessions to the United States.[8] Kim explicitly argues against this line of thought.[9] While the demand for security may have decreased for some states in the post–Cold War era, potential security suppliers also decreased, as the United States became the only viable guarantor of security for states facing down threats in their home regions. As a result, Kim argues that the United States retains much of its previous bargaining power.

Brooks, Ikenberry, and Wohlforth argue that the United States has secured a better bargain on its free trade agreements as a result of its security provision even after the end of the Cold War. The authors conducted interviews with officials involved in both the Bush administration's negotiations of the U.S.-Australia Free Trade Agreement and the Obama administration's negotiations of the U.S.-South Korea Free Trade Agreement; these officials highlighted the impact of U.S. security provisions on the course of these negotiations. For example, they noted that South Korea's desire to enhance security cooperation within the alliance made them more flexible regarding the terms of the agreement, specifically noting impacts on labor, environment, and auto clauses.[10] Brooks, Ikenberry, and Wohlforth also argue that the United States achieved better terms than the European Union achieved in its free trade agreement with South Korea.[11] In addition, Sohn and Koo argue that when the negotiations slowed, South Korean President Roh decided to make concessions to the United States to strengthen security ties and that the catalyst for final ratification was North Korean aggression, specifically the sinking of the *Cheonan* and artillery attacks on Yeon-pyeong Island in 2010.[12]

Outside of the U.S. case, there is further evidence that hegemons can exercise this bargaining leverage. Davis examines the case of the Anglo-Japanese alliance during a period of British hegemony and finds that Britain was able to secure better terms in tariff negotiations by exerting security leverage.[13] Japan proposed an overall increase in tariffs that would extend to Britain, even though Britain's own free trade policies allowed Japanese goods to enter Britain duty-free. Japan did not offer preferential tariffs for any British goods, treating allies and adversaries the same. Early on in communications between the two governments, British officials stressed that negotiations had the potential to damage the existing alliance. As negotiations continued without resolution, the British ambassador stressed that, due to these tariff negotiations, the British government would have to consider increasingly negative public sentiment about Japan when it came time to negotiate the renewal of the alliance in

---

[8] Drezner, 2013.

[9] Kim, 2016.

[10] Brooks, Ikenberry, and Wohlforth, 2013, p. 44.

[11] Brooks and Wohlforth, 2016. Drezner had previously expressed skepticism of this claim (Drezner, 2013, p. 65).

[12] Yul Sohn and Min Gyo Koo, "Securitizing Trade: The Case of the Korea-U.S. Free Trade Agreement," *International Relations of the Asia-Pacific*, Vol. 11, No. 3, 2011, pp. 450–454.

[13] Christina L. Davis, "Linkage Diplomacy: Economic and Security Bargaining in the Anglo-Japanese Alliance, 1902–23," *International Security*, Vol. 33, No. 3, 2009, pp. 170–172.

1910. Japanese Prime Minister Katsura noted how impactful this statement would be in the diet, stressing it would be a very powerful lever in convincing the diet to make concessions. Japan soon accepted the previously proposed agreement offered by Britain.

This leverage has not always been used. Stokes and Waterman note that the United States had not sought to put an end to Japanese mercantilism in the decades following World War II, and it only did so when its economy faced difficulties.[14] Similarly, Davis notes that earlier in the alliance, Britain had concerns about maintaining the security alliance despite being the stronger military power and thus did not respond when the provision of government subsidies allowed Japanese merchants to undercut the prices of those in England.[15] As such, Japan was able to exert leverage through its provision of security, even though it was the militarily weaker power. Further, as Stein suggests, both the United States and Great Britain were willing to accept economic discrimination at times, rather than attempting to utilize military leverage, in their attempts to create a free trade system.[16]

If the United States grants economic benefits to its partners more frequently than it exerts its bargaining leverage, this pathway might ultimately prove ineffective. However, the sole quantitative examination of this question finds no evidence that the United States systematically subordinates its economic goals to support its alliance commitments.[17] Wolford and Kim examine whether alliance partners who have greater economic power are willing to sacrifice economic goals for their allies. They examine cases in which governments reject domestic calls for antidumping duties, which are designed to offset the advantage that foreign firms gain by selling goods at prices below the costs of production while being funded by their national governments. They find that the greater a state's overall market power in comparison with that of their alliance partners (as represented by their share of the total GDP of the two states combined), the more likely they are to reject antidumping petitions, suggesting that economic powers do sacrifice some economic gains in favor of their alliance partners. However, when examining the U.S. case individually, the authors find that this effect does not hold.[18] It is not clear whether this is due to the unique military or economic position of the United States, but it does demonstrate that the United States is not likely to systematically compromise its economic goals in its relationships with allies and partners.

In sum, powerful states have been able to leverage their security provision to extract better terms from their partners, although they occasionally instead sacrifice their economic interests in support of maintaining alliances. While there is little systematic quantitative evidence

---

[14] Stokes and Waterman, 2017, pp. 1047–1049.

[15] Davis, 2009, p. 166. Davis argues that domestic political factors explain the choices of the British government.

[16] Arthur A. Stein, "The Hegemon's Dilemma: Great Britain, the United States, and the International Economic Order," *International Organization*, Vol. 38, No. 2, 1984.

[17] Scott Wolford and Moonhawk Kim, "Alliances and the High Politics of International Trade," *Political Science Research and Methods*, Vol. 5, No. 4, 2017.

[18] Wolford and Kim, 2017, pp. 605–607.

supporting this pathway, a close examination of individual cases does support the hypothesis that, in some cases, the hegemon can leverage its security provision to gain better terms in economic negotiations.

The Effects of Military Engagement on Firm Behavior Have Not Been Explored Empirically

In addition to altering the behavior of foreign governments, U.S. military engagement may alter the behavior of foreign firms. One way that U.S. forward engagement might increase trade and investment between the United States and its partners in peacetime is by altering firms' perceptions about the risk of conflict disrupting economic exchange. If U.S. military engagement reduces the *perceived* risk of conflict, firms in countries that are U.S. allies or that host U.S. forces should be more willing to make the long-term investments necessary to support cross-national exchange.[19] This should make the ally more productive economically and a more attractive partner for U.S. trade and investment.[20]

Given the evidence we found on the impact of military engagement on the outbreak of conflict, we expect that firms will have a lower perceived risk of conflict in the presence of a U.S. alliance or U.S. military personnel. This should lead partner-nation firms to make the domestic investment necessary to engage in greater trade and cross-national investments with other countries generally, but it is not clear the extent to which this might lead to increases in trade and investment with U.S. firms. Existing research has not examined how this change in the perception of the risk of conflict affects the trade and investment relationship between the security provider—the United States—and its partners.

One study looks at a specific implication of risk reduction. U.S. military engagement may impact firm behavior by reducing the likelihood that commerce is intercepted or destroyed en route. If so, this should reduce the insurance premiums that firms pay to ship goods between the United States and the partner. Egel et al. explore this question by studying freight and insurance charges for all U.S. bilateral trade from 1975 to 2004, examining air and water costs individually.[21] The authors do not find any evidence that U.S. security commitments reduce insurance costs with partners and allies. The results of a U.S. presence on shipping costs are inconsistent.[22] While the authors find a significant effect of overall U.S. troop presence in reducing water-transportation costs, they find no significant effect of overall U.S. troop

---

[19] See also Long, 2008.

[20] Heo and Ye, 2019, pp. 234–267.

[21] Egel et al., 2016, chap. 7. The authors use data collected by Hummels, 2007.

[22] The authors find that a forward U.S. presence does reduce trade costs at the regional level; however, that does not directly speak to the pathway considered here.

presence on air-shipping costs.[23] The sum total of results here does not suggest a clear enough picture to draw substantial inferences from a single source.

A second way that U.S. forward engagement might induce firms to increase their level of economic exchange with the United States in peacetime is by altering beliefs about the risk of trade with or investment in the United States. The impact of uncertainty more broadly on firm-level outcomes has been a focus in the economics literature, with uncertainty serving as a major inhibitor of economic activity.[24] When the United States has made a security commitment to a country or when the United States keeps peacetime forces in that country, this should remove some uncertainty about the future course of the broader U.S.-partner relationship.[25]

U.S. and allies' firms may be more likely to engage in trade and investment because they do not fear that political or economic disputes could close markets and prevent exchange.[26] Given their security ties, firms may believe that the United States and its partner are more likely to experience policy convergence and work cooperatively on economic issues in the future, lowering barriers to trade and avoiding costly economic sanctions. Firms in the partner country and the United States are therefore more likely to engage with each other in trade and cross-border investments because they believe the two nations will foster a conducive political-economic environment over the long term.

Military engagement can also reduce uncertainty about the preferences of each side. Through military engagement, personal networks expand across nations, which may allow economic actors to gain information about the domestic preferences of their allies as well as the composition of their economies, thereby overcoming existing barriers to entry in the foreign market.[27]

Despite this strong theoretical motivation to believe that U.S. military engagement may lead foreign firms to have greater confidence in conducting trade and investment with the United States, no existing studies have directly examined how the presence of an alliance or the deployment of military personnel in peacetime might reduce uncertainty. This is a major gap in the literature, as it prevents us from considering how firm-level decisionmaking may be affected by U.S. military engagement.

---

[23] Further, looking at service-specific figures, they find that a U.S. Navy presence and a U.S. Army presence are associated with higher air-shipping costs. However, we note that some of the authors' results may be unstable due to insufficient controls for endogeneity.

[24] See, for example, Scott R. Baker, Nicholas Bloom, and Steven J. Davis, "Measuring Economic Policy Uncertainty," *Quarterly Journal of Economics*, Vol. 131, No. 4, November 2016.

[25] Bagozzi and Landis, 2015; Li and Vashchilko, 2010.

[26] Long, 2008; Long and Leeds, 2006; Jones and Kane, 2012.

[27] For a discussion of these networks, see Michael A. Allen, Michael E. Flynn, Carla Martinez Machain, and Andrew Stravers, "Outside the Wire: U.S. Military Deployments and Public Opinion in Host States," *American Political Science Review*, Vol. 114, No. 2, 2020.

Summary

Ultimately, we find suggestive evidence for the bargaining leverage pathway. While the evidence is not systematic, prominent instances of the United States—and other hegemons—exerting this leverage can be found over time. However, because we cannot draw any conclusions from the current literature about firm behavior, it is not yet possible to truly explain why alliances and a forward military presence have been associated with increases in trade and investment between the United States and its partners. This makes it difficult to inform policy decisions, as we are unable to set firm expectations of which relationships do or could have more significant economic benefits.

CHAPTER 5

Do U.S. Alliances Increase U.S. Economic Welfare by Increasing Trade?

We have discussed at length how empirical analyses of the effects of military engagement on economic outcomes have focused primarily on bilateral changes in measures such as trade and investment. Ultimately, we would like to know how these changes affect U.S. economic welfare. Moreover, we would like to know whether these higher levels of trade are caused by alliances or whether the relationship runs the other direction. As a first step toward answering these key policy questions, this chapter presents our own empirical analysis of one dimension of this broader relationship—the impact of U.S. alliances on U.S. economic welfare through changes in trade in manufactured goods. Using data on global alliances for the period from 1986 to 2006, we find that U.S. involvement in NATO had a modest positive impact on U.S. economic welfare by increasing trade.

To reach this conclusion, we developed a three-step analytical approach, which we discuss in the remainder of this chapter. First, we use global data on alliances and trade to estimate the changes in bilateral trade that result from the formation of an alliance. While this is where most analyses of the economic effect of alliance commitments begin and end, we carry forth this analysis to consider the impact on the U.S. economy as a whole. Second, we translate this change in trade into a measure of the reduction in trade barriers between states that is required to produce the same impact on trade as the formation of an alliance.[1] Finally, we use that measure in a model of global trade in manufactured goods to predict the effect on U.S. economic welfare. This allows us to say more about the broader impact of U.S. alliance commitments on the U.S. economy than do previous studies. We present a simplified discussion of our analysis in this chapter and include a more detailed discussion of our models and results in a technical appendix.

Step 1: Modeling the Effect of Alliances on Bilateral Trade

Data and Empirical Specification

We begin by assessing the relationship between the level of bilateral trade and the presence of a defensive alliance using regression analysis. Trade data come from Yotov et al. and covers

---

[1] This is what is known as a tariff-equivalent measure.

the period from 1986 to 2006.[2] The data include both international trade and domestic sales in manufactured products.[3] Including domestic sales data allows us to incorporate how changes in interstate alliances influence bilateral trade while accounting for competition in domestic markets. Data on alliances come from the Correlates of War Formal Alliances data set. We include a variable that is equal to 1 if two countries have a defensive alliance in a given year, and is equal to 0 otherwise.[4]

Our data look at the relationship between trade and alliances, both across countries and over time. When working with this type of data, we can take a number of steps to isolate the relationship between alliances and trade from factors that may make estimating the relationship more difficult.

Fixed effects. A number of factors may influence both the level of trade between countries and whether the countries have an alliance. For instance, countries that are closer geographically may have a stronger incentive to form defensive alliances against shared threats and may have stronger economic ties than more distant pairs of countries due to lower transportation costs. Similarly, a country's income level may influence its level of trade and its potential for appearing to be an attractive ally to other countries.

To address these potentially confounding factors, we include fixed effects in our regression. First, we include fixed effects to control for all characteristics that are specific to a pair of countries that do not vary over time. Factors like whether countries share a common national language are controlled for by these fixed effects. Second, we include fixed effects to control for all country-specific time-varying factors affecting trade. These effects include factors like GDP, technological productivity, and the state's level of military spending.

Due to the inclusion of fixed effects, our estimate of how trade changes in response to defense alliances is based on whether defense alliances are formed or terminated between the same pair of trade partners over time. The period we study includes the formation of 42 alliances and just six alliance terminations. As a result, our estimates are based largely on the effects of alliance formation, not alliance termination, a point that we will return to in greater depth.

Including fixed effects in our regression does not eliminate all potential sources of bias, specifically from characteristics that vary at the country-pair level over time. For instance, whether two countries have a trade agreement will influence the level of trade between the

---

[2]   The time period of the sample is determined by data availability.

[3]   It has become standard to include intranational trade flows in empirical assessments of trade. Benedikt Heid, Mario Larch, and Yoto V. Yotov, "Estimating the Effects of Non-Discriminatory Trade Policies Within Structural Gravity Models," *Canadian Journal of Economics/Revue canadienne d'économique*, Vol. 21, 2021; Robert C. Feenstra et al., "In Search of the Armington Elasticity," *Review of Economics and Statistics*, Vol. 100, No. 1, 2018; Maria Cipollina and Luca Salvatici, "The Trade Impact of EU Tariff Margins: An Empirical Assessment," *Social Sciences*, Vol. 8, No. 9, 2019; Yoto V. Yotov, Roberta Piermartini, Jose-Antonio Monteiro, and Mario Larch, *An Advanced Guide to Trade Policy Analysis: The Structural Gravity Model Online Revised Version*, Geneva, Switzerland: World Trade Organization and the United Nations, 2016.

[4]   Douglas M. Gibler, *International Military Alliances, 1648–2008*, Washington, D.C.: CQ Press, 2008.

countries and may also influence whether the countries have an alliance, given the evidence that trade may affect alliance decisions. Because the presence of trade agreements between countries varies over time and is potentially related to the presence of both an alliance and bilateral trade, as noted in earlier, its exclusion may bias our results.[5] To remedy this, we include a variable in our regression that captures whether trade partners have an active trade agreement. Data for this variable come from Egger and Larch (2008) and include all forms of trade agreements, including regional agreements and bilateral agreements. The trade agreement variable takes the value of 1 when the countries have some form of trade agreement and 0 otherwise.[6]

Accounting for reverse causality. Even with our fixed effects and additional controls for the presence of trade agreements, we must also consider the potential of reverse causality. As we discussed in Chapter 3, states may form defensive alliances to protect their existing or prospective trade partners. Thus, the direction of the causal relationship between trade and alliances is difficult to assess. To help alleviate this problem, we include the five-year lagged version of the defense agreement variable.[7] That is, we examine changes in trade five years after an alliance is formed. Intuitively, alliances signed five years ago may influence trade, but it is unlikely that changes in bilateral trade five years into the future will influence defense alliances.[8] Further, this structure allows us to consider that defense agreements may take time to have an effect on trade.

Clustered standard errors. Our observations are not independent of one another, since country pairs repeat in the sample over time. That is, trade between the United States and Canada in 2005 is closely related to trade between these states in 2006. As a result, we used clustered standard errors at the importer-exporter level to ensure we are not overestimating our precision.

After making these three adjustments, we have a very simple regression model where bilateral trade is a function of alliances, trade agreements, and fixed effects. We estimate this model using the Pseudo-Poisson Maximum Likelihood (PPML). This method has many of the same properties as the more common linear Ordinary Least Squares regression but

---

[5] For an omitted variable to bias our estimate, the omitted variable must be correlated with the presence of a defense alliance between countries.

[6] We also control for UN General Assembly voting similarity as a robustness check and find our major results are unchanged.

[7] This approach is similar to that used in Bove, Elia, and Sekeris, 2014, which examines the bilateral trade response of military aid and U.S. military presence.

[8] We do not use a shorter lag, such as one year, to avoid capturing anticipated changes in trade. One exception to this is through the potential anticipatory effect, where countries may sign a defense alliance with the expectation that trade may grow in the future. Controlling for our fixed effects and trade agreements, however, we find that trade and a five-year lag of trade are correlated only at 0.4. As additional tests, we estimate the model using a 10-year lag or a 15-year lag in defense alliances. We find that the magnitude of the effect decreases but that it is always substantively large and statistically significant.

provides more consistent estimates in the presence of zero trade flows, which, as Egel et al. note, is an important consideration in the data.[9]

Discussion of Results

Our results suggest that defensive alliances have a large and statistically significant association with bilateral trade, consistent with the existing literature. In our model, we estimate the coefficient (β) on our defensive alliance variable to be 0.58 (with a 95 percent confidence interval of 0.47 to 0.64). For ease of interpretation, we convert the coefficient into a simple percent change using the following formula for a PPML model: $(exp[0.58] - 1 \cdot 100) = 78.6$. In other terms, we find that the presence of a defensive alliance between two countries is associated with a 79 percent increase in bilateral trade, on average.[10]

As with any regression, the results assume that all other factors are held constant. As noted, our model is holding constant national incomes, trade with other countries, and prices. For this reason, the results of the regression model should be thought of as the *partial equilibrium response* because they do not allow other economic factors to adjust to the new level of trade. In contrast, *general equilibrium results*, which we consider next, can be thought of as the "full" economic impact of alliances (through changes in trade) as they reflect these subsequent adjustments (i.e., they capture changes between the old and new equilibria in the economy, which is a product of the reactionary behavior we have described).[11]

Step 2: Calculating How Alliances Change Trade Costs

To calculate the "full" economic impact of alliances through trade, we use what is known as the *structural gravity model*, perhaps the most well-known and most used general equilibrium model of trade. Our general equilibrium model of trade describes bilateral trade between

---

[9] Trade data often contain zero-value trade flows, where the value of trade between countries is too small to measure. When estimating log-linear models of trade, these zero-value trade flows are either omitted or adjusted by using *log* (*trade* + 1). Both methods produce biased estimates while including the zero-valued trade, whereas using a Pseudo-Poisson model produces consistent estimates. Joao Santos Silva and Silvana Tenreyro, "FLEX: Stata Module for Flexible Pseudo Maximum Likelihood Estimation of Models for Doubly-Bounded Data," *Economic Papers*, 2016.

[10] This result is similar to the average found across other studies. For example, Long calculates effects in excess of 100 percent; Mansfield and Bronson calculate estimates of 20–30 percent for states without a regional trade agreement and 120–140 percent for those with such an agreement; and Gowa and Mansfield estimate 50 percent for trade of goods with constant returns to scale and 90 percent for trade of goods with increasing returns to scale. Long, 2008; Long, 2003; Gowa and Mansfield, 2004; Mansfield and Bronson, 1997.

[11] *General equilibrium* refers to a modeling framework in which producers seek to minimize costs and consumers maximize the value of the goods they purchase given their budget constraints, resulting in a competitive equilibrium for producers and consumers.

countries as a function of trade flows and trade costs.[12] *Trade costs* are broadly defined as all costs incurred in getting a good to a final consumer, aside from the production cost of the good itself. For instance, trade costs include, but are not limited to, transportation costs, policy barriers such as tariffs, and information costs. Changes in trade costs between two countries result in changes to bilateral trade. For example, when a tariff is removed, the costs of trade are lower and therefore trade rises.

The change in trade then influences competition in markets, prices, and incomes in the domestic economies of each trading partner. These changes in prices and incomes at the domestic level feed back into the global economic system and can influence trade with all partners. As a result, changes in trade costs between two countries not only affect trade between the countries but also influence trade with third-party countries.[13]

The effect that alliances have on bilateral trade between allies can be thought of as a change in trade costs. There are many ways, at least in theory, that alliances may reduce the cost of cross-border trade. For instance, as we have discussed, alliances are thought to reduce uncertainty about a trading relationship, which, if true, would reduce the cost of engaging in international trade, for example, by lowering costs for insurance, among other risk-reduction measures. Governments of allied countries may also encourage private enterprises to engage in trade with each other, using incentives that explicitly or implicitly reduce transaction costs. There are multiple potential mechanisms by which alliances may reduce the cost of engaging in trade and thus increase trade between members.

Viewing alliances as influencing trade costs provides a new way to think about the results discussed above. Now, the increase in trade we find is a combination of both the effect of alliances on reducing trade costs and the effect of reduced trade costs on trade.[14] The effect of reduced trade costs on trade is well explored in the literature, which has calculated this quantity, on average, to be 4.[15] Using the coefficient derived in the first stage of

---

[12] For example, see Marc J. Melitz, "The Impact of Trade on Intra-Industry Reallocations and Aggregate Industry Productivity," *Econometrica*, Vol. 71, No. 6, 2003; Jonathan Eaton and Samuel Kortum, "Technology, Geography, and Trade," *Econometrica*, Vol. 70, No. 5, 2002. We take advantage of recent developments in the empirical international trade literature and solve the model in changes, rather than in levels, a technique pioneered by Dekel et al. (Eddie Dekel, Matthew O. Jackson, and Asher Wollinsky, "Vote Buying: General Elections," *Journal of Political Economy*, Vol. 116, No. 2, 2008). This allows us to calibrate the model on existing trade and production shares. It also eliminates the need for data on technology levels, endowments of labor or capital, initial trade frictions, or initial prices, which would normally be required in a structural gravity model.

[13] Note that because we have included several sets of fixed effects, we have controlled for the impact of many other trade costs in our estimation of the relationship between alliances and bilateral trade.

[14] The effect of trade costs on trade, which is commonly referred to as trade elasticity, is a theoretical concept that measures how much trade flows respond to changes in trade costs.

[15] Ina Simonovska and Michael E. Waugh, "The Elasticity of Trade: Estimates and Evidence," *Journal of International Economics*, Vol. 92, No. 1, January 1, 2014. Other studies have pointed out that there may be considerable heterogeneity in trade cost elasticities across countries and across products. Jean Imbs and Isabelle Mejean, "Trade Elasticities," *Review of International Economics*, Vol. 25, No. 2, 2017. As a result, empirical analyses of the welfare implications of trade typically report results using a range of trade cost elasticities. We provide this type of sensitivity analysis below.

our analysis (0.58) and this figure, we therefore calculate that alliances reduce trade costs by 13.49 percent. Another way to put this result is that alliances have a similar impact on bilateral trade as the removal of a 13.49 percent tariff.[16]

To put this result in perspective, scholars have estimated that two countries sharing a common currency have an effect on trade that is equivalent to a 26 percent tariff reduction, two countries sharing a common language have an effect on trade that is equivalent to a 12 percent tariff reduction, and a 10-day reduction in travel time between trade partners has an effect on trade that is equivalent to an 8 percent tariff reduction.[17] Thus, our estimated effect suggests that defense alliances have a similar effect on trade as other common reductions in trade barriers.

Step 3: Modeling the Effect of Changing Trade Costs on the U.S. Economy

We place our analysis of the effect of alliances in reducing trade costs into our general equilibrium model, which allows prices and incomes for all states to adjust to the new level of trade. This permits us to evaluate how economic welfare in the United States, measured in terms of consumer purchasing power, differs under alternative alliance scenarios.[18] As before, we estimate this model using PPML.

Scenario

Since the ongoing value of NATO has been a point of debate in the grand strategy literature, we consider how U.S. domestic economic welfare would have changed in 2006, the final year of our data, if the United States had exited NATO five years prior.[19] Given Canada's geographic proximity—as well as the interlinked homeland defense missions that Canada and the United States currently manage, for example, through the North American Aerospace

---

[16] See the appendix for an explanation of this calculation.

[17] Hiau Looi Kee, Alessandro Nicita, and Marcelo Olarreaga, "Estimating Trade Restrictiveness Indices," *Economic Journal*, Vol. 119, January 1, 2009; Hummels, 2007; James E. Anderson and Eric van Wincoop, "Trade Costs," *Journal of Economic Literature*, Vol. 42, No. 3, September 1, 2004.

[18] Our measure of welfare, which we refer to as consumer purchasing power, is the ratio of wages to average consumer prices. This ratio is technically the real wage and measures the buying power of consumer income. The same gauge is commonly used to measure welfare in general equilibrium trade analysis. Lorenzo Caliendo and Fernando Parro, "Estimates of the Trade and Welfare Effects of NAFTA," *Review of Economic Studies*, Vol. 82, No. 1, 2015; Costas Arkolakis, Arnaud Costinot, and Andrés Rodríguez-Clare, "New Trade Models, Same Old Gains?" *American Economic Review*, Vol. 102, No. 1, 2012; Scott L. Baier, Yoto V. Yotov, and Thomas Zylkin, "On the Widely Differing Effects of Free Trade Agreements: Lessons from Twenty Years of Trade Integration," *Journal of International Economics*, Vol. 116, January 1, 2019.

[19] Due to our lag structure, this means exiting NATO in 2001, an unlikely event in the real world. However, this allows us to use the most up-to-date trade data in our sample.

Defense Command—we assume the United States would maintain an alliance with Canada even if it withdrew from its commitments to countries in Europe. We leave other defense alliances, both within NATO and elsewhere, unchanged.

Discussion of Results

Our analysis finds that in this scenario, U.S. welfare (as measured by purchasing power) declined by approximately 0.4 percent relative to actual U.S. welfare in 2006.[20] This is a relatively modest change, but alliances are not specifically designed to impact U.S. economic welfare.[21] Further, this does not examine how effects may persist in future years. In the absence of further policy interventions, this decline in welfare would be expected to persist.[22] Additionally, our analysis focuses only on trade in manufactured goods, and trade volume in manufactured goods between the United States and its NATO allies is relatively low.[23] Incorporating trade in services and raw materials would likely result in larger welfare changes.[24]

Scholars have previously estimated that China entering the WTO increased average U.S. welfare by 6.7 percent and that U.S. welfare would have been 6.4 percent higher if all border barriers among countries in the Organization for Economic Co-operation and Development (OECD) were eliminated.[25] The effects of these changes are much larger than our estimates, which tracks with a commonsense understanding of these events. For instance, China entering the WTO was an enormous economic shock to the global economy, because goods from the world's largest producer become cheaper in global markets. However, our welfare estimates are larger than the estimate of the welfare impact of North American

---

[20] Constructing a 95 percent confidence interval, the lower bound of this estimate is a 0.04 percent decrease, and the upper bound is a 0.6 percent decrease.

[21] The model also produces a welfare change for other countries. Due to trade diversion away from non-Canada NATO members, consumer purchasing power in Mexico, Canada, and non-NATO European countries like Ireland, Austria, and Sweden would have been higher in the counterfactual. NATO members (excluding those in Canada) see a decline in consumer purchasing power in the counterfactual, although most of these changes are relatively small compared to those in the United States.

[22] As a result, this functions as a lower bound on the effect on U.S. welfare.

[23] Most U.S. trade in manufactured goods is with East and South Asian countries as opposed to with NATO members. In the economic model, welfare changes depend on initial trade shares. The model predicts that trade flows that are small in the baseline should remain small after a defense alliance changes. Thus, even a large shift in the trade of manufactured goods between the United States and its NATO allies will have a more muted effect on U.S. welfare overall.

[24] Egel et al., for example, scale up their estimates based on the composition of trade into trade in goods and trade in services at the time of their analysis, resulting in a 28 percent increase in their estimate, as trade in goods represented 72 percent of overall trade. Using 2021 data, this would result in a 22 percent increase in our estimate. Egel et al., 2016; U.S. Census, *U.S. International Trade in Goods and Services*, May 4, 2022.

[25] For the WTO analysis, see Lorenzo Caliendo, Maximiliano Dvorkin, and Fernando Parro, *The Impact of Trade on Labor Market Dynamics*, Cambridge, Mass.: National Bureau of Economic Research, WR-21149, May 1, 2015. For the OECD analysis, see Anderson and Wincoop, 2004.

Free Trade Agreement (NAFTA), which is generally estimated to have been less than 0.2 percent for the United States and has been noted by analysts as having a modest impact on the U.S. economy.[26]

While we focus on changes in welfare, the model also allows us to evaluate how trade would have looked in the counterfactual scenario. We find that exports from the United States to the average non-Canada NATO member would have been approximately 35 percent lower and that U.S. imports from the average non-Canada NATO member would have been approximately 37 percent lower in 2006 if the United States had exited NATO five years prior.

Robustness of the Result and Areas for Future Research

It is important to consider how robust our results are. Our analysis assumes that a 1 percent reduction in trade costs leads to a 4 percent increase in trade. While this assumption is established by the literature, we perform additional analyses to assess how welfare changes respond if the relationship is somewhat different than we assume. Prominent estimates of the effect of trade costs on trade across countries and products range from approximately –20 percent to –2 percent, so we use these values as a benchmark.[27] We find the range of welfare effects to be 0.1 percent to 1 percent across this range. However, in each instance, the United States suffers a statistically significant loss in economic welfare.[28] For any assumption about trade costs and trade in this range, the bottom line is the same: withdrawing from an alliance has a moderate, harmful effect on U.S. economic welfare.

Our findings also have limitations that suggest caveats and areas for future research. First, we note that in our analysis, we do not estimate the effect of alliance formation and alliance termination separately. Since most of the changes in alliances we examine are cases of alliance formation rather than alliance termination, we are largely assuming that the gains from trade due to alliance formation are equivalent to the losses from the trade when alliances end, an assumption that pervades previous work on this topic as well. There has not been research assessing the extent to which this assumption is valid. The economic effects of alliance termination should therefore be further explored moving forward.

Future research in this area should also focus on expanding this analysis. As we have stated, the first stage of our analysis returns an average effect for all alliances around the world between 1986 and 2006. Future analysis should consider other time periods and the possibility that the relationship between alliances and economic benefits varies as interna-

---

[26] Yotov et al., 2016; Joseph B. Steinberg, "The Macroeconomic Impact of NAFTA Termination," *Canadian Journal of Economics/Revue canadienne d'économique*, Vol. 53, No. 2, 2020; Caliendo and Parro, 2015; M. Angeles Villareal and Ian F. Fergusson, *NAFTA at 20: Overview and Trade Effects*, Washington, D.C.: Congressional Research Service, 2014.

[27] Imbs and Mejean, 2017.

[28] We note that the results remain significant; additional robustness checks including the use of year fixed effects and clustering standard errors at the destination-year and origin-year levels (two-way clustering).

tional conditions vary across time. Analysts should also consider the U.S. case in depth. It is possible that U.S. alliances may be different from the average alliance. If the effect of U.S. alliance formation on trade were to be greater (or less) than that of the average alliance, our welfare calculations would be lower (or higher) than they are in actuality.[29] Finally, as we have noted at length, more research is needed to identify the specific mechanisms through which alliances influence trade. Our approach models the net effect of alliances but is silent on specific mechanisms.

Summary

Our analysis extends past intermediate economic effects, which have been the focus of previous research, to look at a more fundamental measure of interest—U.S. economic welfare. We find evidence that U.S. participation in a specific alliance community—NATO—had a modest impact on U.S. economic welfare by increasing trade in manufactured goods. While a deeper examination of the connection between U.S. military engagement and U.S. economic welfare is necessary to understand the true economic benefits of forward U.S. engagement, we provide both the initial first step in this analysis and a guidepost of how scholars should move the literature forward.

---

[29] However, we do note that the results in the first stage of our analysis are similar in magnitude to estimates in a previous study of the United States (Egel et al., 2016).

CHAPTER 6

Findings and Conclusion

Advocates of U.S. military engagement contend that U.S. military hegemony has allowed the United States to extract economic benefits from the system, while advocates of restraint reject the claim that the United States extensively benefits from military hegemony. While we cannot fully adjudicate these claims, through our analysis of the literature and our independent research, we are able to bring a significant amount of evidence to bear on the subject.

Findings

U.S. Alliances Have Had a Modest but Positive Impact on U.S. Economic Welfare by Increasing Peacetime Trade

Scholars have previously found that alliances are associated with an increase in bilateral trade, including in the case of the United States. These analyses do not allow us to say definitively how U.S. economic welfare—the true outcome of interest—responds to shifts in bilateral trade and FDI with allied countries. We take a first step in addressing this disconnect by examining how military engagement affects U.S. economic welfare. Our analysis finds that the United States would have experienced a roughly 0.4 percent decline in consumer purchasing power in 2006 had it exited NATO five years prior rather than sustaining its NATO commitments. This change in U.S. welfare is relatively modest, but its impact is similar to that of a regional trade agreement such as NAFTA and does not examine the extent to which this decline may carry forward over time. Further, our analysis focuses only on trade in manufactured goods. Analyses that also incorporate trade in services and raw materials would likely result in larger welfare changes.

It Is Not Clear Whether Increases in Trade and Investment Associated with U.S. Alliances Would Be Lost If These Relationships Were Renegotiated or Ended

The economic benefits created by an alliance or U.S. forward presence may not be entirely lost when an alliance terminates.[1] It is possible that economic agreements signed and relationships established after alliance creation are "sticky," meaning they can outlive the end of the alliance

---

[1]   Cooperative international regimes, once created and widely accepted among states, tend to persist even without active intervention by the hegemon. Robert O. Keohane, *After Hegemony: Cooperation and Discord in the World Political Economy*, Princeton, N.J.: Princeton University Press, 2005.

itself. This possibility is important when considering how to apply the empirical patterns noted above to policy decisions about alliance termination. For example, our analysis examines a counterfactual in which the United States exited NATO, while Egel et al. construct a counterfactual scenario in which the United States reduced its real-world security commitments by 50 percent. Each analysis seeks to better understand the potential impact of a proposed reduction of U.S. commitments on trade and to find substantial effects. However, each analysis assumes that the net gains from trade due to U.S. security commitments would be equal to the net losses in the absence of those commitments.[2] Scholars have not, however, examined this assumption. In the meantime, therefore, policymakers should consider the possibility that the economic effects of alliance termination may be smaller than current studies suggest.

U.S. Alliances Reduce the Likelihood of War, Though the Impact of Foreign Wars on the U.S. Economy Needs Further Research

We find strong and consistent evidence that, on average, states with alliances are less likely to be involved in conflict. Further, studies on the conditions under which this relationship is strongest suggest that this general finding likely applies to the U.S. case. This means that U.S. alliances likely prevent conflicts that disrupt some international trade and investment. However, it remains unclear how much foreign conflicts affect the U.S. economy in particular. This is because existing studies have only focused on intermediate economic outcomes, such as bilateral trade, rather than economic growth, and they have not considered how U.S. firms might adapt by finding new partners, domestically or abroad.

The Impact of a U.S. Presence on Economic Outcomes in Peacetime Is Underexplored

While a number of studies analyze the effects of alliances on economic outcomes in peacetime, very few scholars have examined the impact of a U.S. presence on either trade or investment, let alone economic welfare. We found only three studies that look at these relationships, two examining the relationship between a U.S. forward presence and U.S. trade and one examining the relationship between a U.S. forward presence and investment. While these studies do suggest that a U.S. presence is associated with an increase in bilateral trade and investment, more work must be done to examine the robustness of these results.

Recommendations for Future Research

Examine the Effects of U.S. Military Engagement on Economic Welfare in Greater Depth

Our welfare analysis in Chapter 5 is a first step in quantifying the size of the benefit of military engagement to the U.S. economy. We consider the impact of U.S. alliances on U.S. economic

---

[2] This is not strictly true, as some cases of alliance removal are present in each data set.

welfare, but future research should consider the effects of U.S. forward presence. Similarly, while we examine the effect of U.S. alliances on economic welfare through increasing trade, we do not examine the impact of additional pathways such as increased investment, which could potentially increase the economic benefits of alliances. In addition, future research could consider how the effects of U.S. military engagement might vary by region or industry.

Future research could also consider the distributional effects of U.S. military engagement. Certain groups may benefit or lose disproportionately from shifts in alliance relationships or military posture. The distributional effects of changes in U.S. military engagement may factor into how much policymakers weigh the economic benefits of alliances against other factors. For example, the Biden administration has repeatedly emphasized its desire to craft a foreign policy for the middle class.[3] So, if the increases in consumer purchasing power uncovered by our model were concentrated within the middle class, this administration might place a higher weight on these benefits than another administration would.

Examine the Mechanism by Which U.S. Military Engagement Affects Bilateral Economic Relationships

Our findings suggest that U.S. alliances increase bilateral trade. We discuss a number of possible pathways by which this increase may occur. It may be that firms perceive stability in the relationship between allies and therefore engage in more trade. Alternatively, allies may adopt policies to incentivize firms to trade more. The United States may also use its security guarantees as leverage in bargaining to force U.S. allies to make concessions in economic negotiations. However, the relative importance of independent firm behavior, U.S. leverage, or other factors is not clear from the existing literature. Knowing more about the mechanism by which trade would likely increase would help policymakers understand how and where changes in U.S. military engagement would be expected to have the biggest impact on U.S. economic welfare.

Explore How Other Policy Tools, Such as Trade and Investment Agreements, Compare with Alliances in Affecting Trade

As discussed above, policymakers do not usually talk about U.S. military engagement as an economic tool. Still, alliances and posture choices can have economic effects. Therefore, if policymakers were considering reductions in U.S. military engagement, they might wish to consider economic policies that could offset some of the effects of the change in security policies. Today, it is difficult to assess the relative effects of economic inducements and military engagement, due to the lack of directly comparable research on this subject. While we discuss how the effects of alliances compare with some prominent trade agreements in Chapter 5,

---

[3] Joseph R. Biden, Jr., "Why America Must Lead Again: Recusing U.S. Foreign Policy After Trump," *Foreign Affairs*, Vol. 99, 2020.

future research could further explore the similarities and differences in the effects of economic and security policy changes.

Assess the Extent to Which Ending Alliances Decreases Bilateral Trade

As noted, the economic benefits created by an alliance or U.S. forward presence may not be entirely lost when an alliance terminates. Our examination of U.S. welfare, bilateral trade, and U.S. alliances assumes that the gains from trade due to alliance formation are equivalent to the losses from the trade when alliances end. This assumption also pervades previous work on this subject. However, quantitative and qualitative research should examine cases of alliance termination and assess the extent to which economic relationships change. This research should compare the effects of forming and ending alliances.

Assess How Easily the U.S. Economy Can Adapt to Disruptions Caused by Foreign Wars

In the debate about U.S. grand strategy, some strategists call for fewer U.S. alliances, which may increase the risk of war in some cases. If the United States were to remain a non-belligerent in such wars, its economy could still be affected. Both sides in the grand strategy debate acknowledge that conflicts can create adjustment costs, while disagreeing on how deep and long-lasting these effects will be. The existing literature does not provide enough information for us to assess how quickly firms can adapt in wartime, especially in today's globalized world. Future research should therefore consider these adjustment costs. Existing research suggests that future analysis will need to look beyond large wars in the distant past (e.g., World War I), because the effects of war on economic exchange may change with time. Moreover, existing research suggests that the effects of war on economic exchange is highly context-dependent, so future research will need to consider the U.S. case in particular, not just average global effects.

Conclusion

Decisions about U.S. alliances and forward military presence should be based on a range of factors beyond potential economic benefits. We therefore do not make recommendations about whether or how the United States should change its security policies. Instead, we describe the observable economic benefits associated with U.S. military engagement that should inform a broader assessment of the value of an engaged U.S. grand strategy.

There is evidence that U.S. military engagement has historically helped the United States economy by promoting international commerce. The best evidence suggests that these results are positive and on the order of a regional free trade agreement. The extent to which these results will hold in the future is an important question to be explored in greater depth to allow policymakers to better understand the economic consequences of their policy choices.

Statistical Analysis of U.S. Alliances and Economic Welfare

In this appendix, we describe in greater detail our empirical analysis of the impact of U.S. alliances on U.S. economic welfare through changes in trade, which we described in simplified form in Chapter 5.

Measuring Economic Welfare

In our analysis, we operationalize economic welfare as the change in purchasing power in each country. The intuition behind this way of measuring welfare is simple: countries are better off when their purchasing power grows. We calculate the change in welfare as the change in national expenditures relative to the change in national prices. This method is commonly used to measure the welfare response to changes in trade policy.[1]

Theoretical Framework

In estimating the effect of alliances on economic welfare, we begin with a gravity model of bilateral trade. Specifically, we begin with a common gravity model in which we consider trade to be a function of a country's expenditures, including consumption, investment, and transfer payments; technology levels; production costs, such as the costs of labor and raw materials; trade costs; and the substitutability of goods from different geographical origins.[2] This model is formalized in the following gravity equation, derived from the structural

---

[1] For instance, see James E. Anderson and Yoto V. Yotov, "Terms of Trade and Global Efficiency Effects of Free Trade Agreements, 1990–2002," *Journal of International Economics*, Vol. 99, 2016; Baier, Yotov, and Zylkin, 2019; Arnaud Costinot and Andrés Rodríguez-Clare, "Chapter 4: Trade Theory with Numbers: Quantifying the Consequences of Globalization," in Gita Gopinath, Elhanan Helpman, and Kenneth Rogoff, eds., *Handbook of International Economics*, Vol. 4, New York: Elsevier, 2014.

[2] Eaton and Kortum, 2002; Anderson and Wincoop, 2004; Baier, Yotov, and Zylkin, 2019.

model of trade that was popularized by Eaton and Kortum (2002) and Anderson and van Wincoop (2003):

$$X_{ijt} = \frac{A_{it} w_{it}^{-\theta} \tau_{ijt}^{-\theta}}{\Sigma_k A_{kt} w_{kt}^{-\theta} \tau_{kjt}^{-\theta}} E_{jt}. \qquad (1)$$

Here, X_{ij} is the value of trade between countries i and j, A_i is a measure of the level of technology in country i, w_i is the production cost in country i, $E_j \equiv \Sigma_i X_{ij}$ is the total expenditure in country j, and $\tau_{ij} \geq 1$ is a vector of iceberg trade costs; the subscript t denotes values that correspond to a particular year.[3] As is typical in models of trade, goods from different origins are considered imperfect substitutes for each other, and the term θ governs this substitutability.[4] Following the literature, we simplify the model by assuming that labor is the only factor of production.[5] The total expenditure in j can be represented as the sum of labor income and trade imbalances, $E_j = w_j L_j + D_j$.

Partial Equilibrium Analysis

Our first step in analyzing the effect of alliances on trade is a partial equilibrium analysis in which we consider the effect of a given policy change on the markets that are *directly* affected. This partial equilibrium analysis allows us to predict the change in bilateral trade in response to changes in defense alliances.

From an empirical perspective, the primary concern of a partial equilibrium analysis based on equation (1) is to estimate the response of trade between countries i and j to changes in combined trade costs (τ_{ijt}). A common approach to estimating the trade response to trade barriers in (1) is by estimating a three-way gravity regression with PPML.[6] The first step in deriving an empirical specification is to note that equation (1) can be represented as follows:

$$X_{ijt} = exp\left(lnA_{it} w_{it}^{-\theta} + ln\frac{E_{jt}}{P_{jt}^{-\theta}} + ln\tau_{ijt}^{-\theta}\right) + e_{ijt}, \text{ where } P_{jt}^{-\theta} = \Sigma_k A_{kt} w_{kt}^{-\theta} \tau_{kjt}^{-\theta}.$$

---

[3] Per Samuelson, trade costs are modeled, as in the transport of ice: we assume some portion of the goods being transported melt along the way, and thus transport costs represent the costs of producing these "melted" goods. Paul A. Samuelson, "The Transfer Problem and Transport Costs, II: Analysis of Effects of Trade Impediments," *Economic Journal*, Vol. 64, No. 254, 1954.

[4] Anderson and Wincoop, 2004; Melitz, 2003; Baier, Yotov, and Zylkin, 2019.

[5] This is another common assumption made in many trade models (see Yotov et al., 2016; Anderson and Wincoop, 2004; Melitz, 2003; Eaton and Kortum, 2002). The assumption is made to simplify calculations, but relaxing it does not alter the models' conclusions. Generally, labor can be thought of as a country's endowments, which include labor, capital, and intermediate goods.

[6] Santos Silva and Tenreyro, 2016, show that estimates from the log-linear specification of the gravity equation can produce biased estimates of elasticities due to the presence of zero-value trade flows. As a robustness check, we find that the empirical results using both PPML and a log-linear specification are not significantly different. However, we rely on the PPML estimates due to the desirable properties of the estimator.

Next, we replace the country-specific terms ($lnA_{it}w_{it}^{-\theta}$ and $ln\frac{E_{jt}}{P_{jt}^{-\theta}}$) with country-year fixed effects. We also include country-pair fixed effects to control for the time-invariant components in the vector of trade costs ($ln\tau_{ijt}^{-\theta}$). This results in the following specification:

$$X_{ijt} = exp[\alpha_{ij} + \alpha_{jt} + \alpha_{it} + -\theta ln\tau_{ijt}] + e_{ijt}.$$

Fixed effects for trade partner or dyad (α_{ij}), exporter year (α_{jt}), and importer year (α_{it}) are thus included. This robust set of fixed effects controls for a number of potential confounding factors. For example, common variables in the gravity model, like the distance between trade partners, is controlled for by the pair fixed effect in all instances in which distance between trade partners does not shift. All time-varying exporter- or importer-specific factors are also accounted for by the exporter-year and importer-year fixed effects. This includes elements of the trade model we have specified—technology, expenditures, and production costs—which do not vary within the same country in the same year.

As we note in the full report, including these fixed effects in our regression does not eliminate potential sources of bias from characteristics that vary at the country-pair level over time. We suggest that whether two countries have a trade agreement will influence the level of trade between the countries and may also influence whether the countries have an alliance; given the evidence that trade may affect alliance decisions, this potentially biases our results. We therefore include a variable in our regression that captures whether trade partners have an active trade agreement.

The vector of trade costs is often modeled as an exponential function of various factors that are hypothesized to influence trade.[7] For our purposes, trade costs may be expressed as $\tau_{ijt} = exp[\gamma_1 Defense_{ijt} + \gamma_2 RTA_{ijt}]$, where $Defense_{ijt}$ is a variable that corresponds to whether countries i and j have a defense alliance in year t, and RTA_{ijt} corresponds to regional trade agreements. When the expression for trade costs is inserted into the regression above, the result is the following:

$$X_{ijt} = exp[\alpha_{ij} + \alpha_{jt} + \alpha_{it} + \beta_1 Defense_{ijt} + \beta_2 RTA_{ijt}] + e_{ijt}. \tag{2}$$

Note that equation (2) allows for an estimate of the structural direct-trade impact of changes in defense agreements and trade agreements. However, in both cases, the estimated parameter on these variables is also a function of the trade elasticity (θ) and of the elasticity of trade costs with respect to defense alliances (γ_1) and trade agreements (γ_2); specifically, $\beta_z = -\theta\gamma_z$, $z = 1,2$.

Given the nonlinearity of the model, interpreting coefficients in the PPML model requires a transformation. Specifically, a coefficient may be interpreted as a percent change with the following calculation: $(exp[\widehat{\beta_z}] - 1) \times 100$. Similarly, interpreting the parameter γ_z as a percentage change requires first isolating the parameter and then exponentiating: $(exp[\widehat{\beta_z/-\theta}] - 1) \times 100$.

The country-pair fixed effect means that the variation used to identify the coefficients in equation (2) must come from changes within pairs over time. Thus, the coefficient on defense

---

[7] For instance, see Anderson and Wincoop, 2004.

alliances is estimated based on variation in the status of defense alliances between trade partners in a given year, and the coefficient on regional trade agreements is based on countries entering and exiting trade agreements with each other over time. The exporter-year and importer-year fixed effects purge the regression of country-year-specific variation that may contribute to the number of defense alliances or trade agreements that a country is a member of across all partners. We cluster our errors at the country-pair level when estimating equation (2).

Data

Following the theoretical description above, the empirical analysis begins by estimating the partial-equilibrium effect and then follows the steps outlined above to calculate the welfare implications of a specific counterfactual scenario. This section describes the data we use in our analysis.

Our trade data come from Yotov et al. and contain information on trade and production in manufacturing between 70 countries for the period of 1986 to 2006.[8] The data include both international trade and domestic sales in manufactured products.[9] Including domestic sales data allows us to incorporate how changes in interstate alliances influence bilateral trade while accounting for competition in domestic markets.

Data on alliances come from the Correlates of War Formal Alliances data set. We include a variable that is equal to 1 if two countries have a defensive alliance in a given year, and 0 otherwise.[10] As we discuss in the report, we must also address potential reverse-causality issues. States may form defense alliances to protect their existing trade partners, for example. Thus, the contemporaneous response of trade to defense alliances is difficult to interpret. To help alleviate these issues, our preferred approach is to use a five-year lagged version of the defense-agreement variable; the motivation behind this approach is that while alliances signed five years prior may influence trade, it is improbable that bilateral trade changes in five years' time influence alliance decisions today. As additional tests, we estimate equation (2) using a 10-year lag or a 15-year lag in defense alliances.

Data on trade agreements come from Egger and Larch (2008) and include all forms of trade agreements, including regional agreements and bilateral agreements.[11] The trade-agreement variable takes the value 1 when the countries have some form of trade agreement and is 0 otherwise.[12]

---

[8] The time period of the sample is determined by data availability.

[9] We note that it has become standard to include intranational trade flows in empirical assessments of trade. Heid, Larch, and Yotov, 2021; Feenstra et al., 2018; Cipollina and Salvatici, 2019; Yotov et al., 2016.

[10] Gibler, 2008.

[11] Egger and Pfaffermayr, 2004.

[12] We also control for UN General Assembly voting similarity as a robustness check and find our major results are unchanged. Michael A Bailey, Anton Strezhnev, and Erik Voeten, "Estimating Dynamic State Preferences from United Nations Voting Data," *Journal of Conflict Resolution*, Vol. 61, No. 2, 2017.

The results are shown in Table A.1. The results across specifications suggest that defense alliances have an economically large and statistically meaningful association with bilateral trade. In our preferred specification with a five-year lag in the alliance variable, we find that the presence of a defensive alliance between two countries is associated with an increase in trade between the countries of 79 percent, on average, which is calculated as $(exp[0.58] - 1) \cdot 100 = 78.6$. When a longer lag in defense alliances is used, the magnitude of the relationship declines, although it remains relatively large and statistically significant.

Recall that the estimated coefficient on the defense-alliance variable is $\beta_1 = -\theta\gamma_1$, where θ is the trade elasticity (assumed to be $\theta = 4$), and γ_1 is the elasticity of trade costs with respect to changes in defense alliances.[13] This elasticity, when expressed in percentage terms, is also commonly referred to as the ad valorem tariff equivalent.[14] It represents how large of a tariff (or subsidy) would be required to produce an equivalent response in bilateral trade. Also recall that, given the nonlinearity of the model, interpreting the parameter γ_1 as a percent change requires the following transformation: $(exp[\widehat{\beta_z/-\theta}] - 1) \times 100$. Thus, for our preferred specification with a five-year lagged defense-alliance variable, the ad valorem tariff equivalent

TABLE A.1
Estimates of Equation (2)

	(1)	(2)	(3)	(4)
$Defense_{ijt}$	0.833***			
	(0.0533)			
$Defense_{ijt-5}$		0.579***		
		(0.041)		
$Defense_{ijt-10}$			0.472***	
			(0.042)	
$Defense_{ijt-15}$				0.288***
				(0.030)
RTA_{ijt}	0.520***	0.536***	0.551***	0.550***
	(0.077)	(0.076)	(0.076)	(0.076)
Observations	99,708	99,708	99,708	99,708
Log-likelihood	−12.16	−12.16	−12.16	−12.16

NOTE: This table displays the results from estimating equation (2). All columns include pair, exporter-year, and importer-year fixed effects. The outcome in all columns is the value of trade between regions i and j in year t. The variable $Defense_{ijt}$ is a dummy variable that takes the value 1 if states i and j have a defense alliance in year t. The variable RTA_{ijt} is a dummy variable that takes the value 1 if i and j have a regional trade agreement in year t. Errors are clustered at the exporter-importer level. Stars indicate level of significance: * $p < 0.1$, ** $p < 0.05$, *** $p < 0.01$.

---

[13] Note that in equation (1), the trade elasticity enters the model as a negative. Thus, while the trade elasticity is assumed to equal 4, it enters the model as −4.

[14] For example, see Kee, Nicita, and Olarreaga, 2009. Céline Carrère and Jaime De Melo, "Non-Tariff Measures: What Do We Know, What Might Be Done?" *Journal of Economic Integration*, Vol. 26, No. 1, 2011.

of a defense alliance is $\left(exp\left[\left(\frac{0.58}{-4}\right) - 1\right]\right) \cdot 100 = -13.49.$[15] This puts the ad valorem tariff equivalent of a defense alliance in line with the average nontariff barrier for manufactured goods, as found in Kee, Nicita, and Olarreaga (2009).

General Equilibrium Analysis

We next turn our attention to the welfare effects of changes in defense alliances. The partial equilibrium response estimated in equation (2) can be extended to evaluate the general equilibrium changes in welfare that result from changes in trade barriers. Note that with estimates of β_1—produced by estimating equation (2)—and an assumption about the value of the trade elasticity (θ), we can predict the change in bilateral trade in response to changes in defense alliances. However, as a traditional gravity model posits, changes in trade costs (and as a result, prices) will have downstream effects in labor markets. Similarly, changes in prices will influence price indices and create trade diversion toward/away from third-party countries. This trade diversion will lead to changes in wages and price indices in third countries as well.

Our general equilibrium analysis will follow the trade model specified in equation (1). We assume first that, in equilibrium, markets clear and there is neither excess supply nor demand. Practically, that means that the total amount of output produced in a country is equal to its expenditures on goods produced, adjusting for trade imbalances. That is, each country's expenditures are equal to the labor they produce and the wages that labor receives. The market-clearing condition for such a model is given by

$$w_i L_i = \sum_j \frac{A_i w_i^{-\theta} \tau_{ij}^{-\theta}}{\sum_k A_k w_k^{-\theta} \tau_{kj}^{-\theta}} (w_j L_j + D_j) \quad \forall i,j. \tag{3}$$

The system of equations in (3) states that the total amount of output produced in country i ($w_i L_i$) is equal to the total amount of expenditures on goods produced in i ($\sum_j \frac{A_i w_i^{-\theta} \tau_{ij}^{-\theta}}{\sum_k A_k w_k^{-\theta} \tau_{kj}^{-\theta}} (w_j L_j + D_j)$). We also allow trade imbalances ($D_j = E_j - w_j L_j$), which, following Baier, Yotov, and Zylkin (2019), enter the model linearly.

Using the exact-hat algebra from Dekle, Eaton, and Kortum (2007), solving the system of equations represented in equation (3) in changes rather than levels eliminates the need for information on technology levels, endowments, initial trade frictions, or initial wages.[16]

---

[15] This method of interpreting the tariff equivalent of nontariff trade barriers is also performed in other studies that use the PPML gravity Computable General Equilibrium framework. For instance, see José De Sousa, Thierry Mayer, and Soledad Zignago, "Market Access in Global and Regional Trade," *Regional Science and Urban Economics*, Vol. 42, No. 6, 2012; Yotov et al., 2016.

[16] Robert Dekle, Jonathan Eaton, and Samuel Kortum, "Unbalanced Trade," *American Economic Review*, Vol. 97, No. 2, 2007.

Denote the change in a variable relative to its initial value with a hat, $\widehat{w}_i = w_i'/w_i$. The equilibrium in changes can be expressed as

$$Y_i\widehat{w}_i = \widehat{w}_i^{-\theta} \sum_j \frac{\pi_{ij}\widehat{\tau}_{ij}^{-\theta}}{\widehat{P}_j^{-\theta}} (Y_j\widehat{w}_j + D_j) \quad \forall(i,j). \tag{4}$$

Here, $\pi_{ij} = X_{ij}/E_j$ is the sum of trade between i and j as a fraction of total expenditures in j, or the trade share. The term

$$\widehat{P}_j = [\sum_k \pi_{kj}\widehat{w_k}^{-\theta}\widehat{\tau}_{kj}^{-\theta}]^{-1/\theta} \tag{5}$$

describes changes in prices in each country (i.e., the change in the price index). The terms Y_i and Y_j in (4) are country-specific baseline output levels. The term $\widehat{\tau}_{ij}^{-\theta}$ represents the change in trade costs due to changes in defense alliances (i.e., the counterfactual trade costs relative to the baseline trade costs). The equilibrium of the economy is given by a solution of equations (4) and (5) for changes in wages ($\widehat{w}_i$) and indices ($\widehat{P}_j$), or the change in price levels that allows markets to clear.[17]

Solving the model requires only initial trade shares (π_{ij}), national output (Y_i), expenditure levels (E_j), and a value for the trade elasticity (θ). We use the last year available in the data to construct the baseline and follow the literature in assuming that the trade elasticity is $\theta = 4$.[18] To solve the model, we use the four-step algorithm developed by Baier, Yotov, and Zylkin (2019), which requires the normalization that world output remains constant in the counterfactual scenario.[19] This normalization is required because trade volumes are in nominal terms.

With changes in wages in hand, we can construct $\widehat{E}_i = (Y_i\widehat{w}_i + D_i)/E_i$, which is the equilibrium change in total expenditures. Then, the following measure can be constructed:

$$\widehat{W}_i = \frac{\widehat{E}_i}{\widehat{P}_i}. \tag{6}$$

Equation (6) is the change in welfare in country i, which is calculated as the change in national expenditures relative to the change in national prices. As discussed, this is commonly used to measure the welfare response to changes in trade policy, since countries are better off when their purchasing power grows.

General Equilibrium Analysis Results

Now that we have estimated the elasticity of trade with respect to defense alliances, as shown in **column 3** of Table A.1, we turn our attention to the general equilibrium response to changes in defense alliances. Using the model described by equations (3) and (4), we explore

---

[17] For proof that this model has a unique solution defined by wages and prices, see Dekle, Eaton, and Kortum, 2007, and Fernando Alvarez and Robert E. Lucas, Jr., "General Equilibrium Analysis of the Eaton-Kortum Model of International Trade," *Journal of Monetary Economics*, Vol. 54, No. 6, 2007.

[18] Simonovska and Waugh, 2014.

[19] See the full description of the four-step algorithm in the GE Gravity package. Thomas Zylkin, "GE_GRAVITY: Stata Module to Solve a Simple General Equilibrium One Sector Armington-CES Trade Model," 2019.

our counterfactual scenario of interest. We examine the welfare implications of the United States terminating its defense alliances with all NATO members except for Canada. In this scenario, we leave all other alliances and trade agreements unchanged.

To account for the fact that the partial equilibrium elasticities (β_1 and β_2) are estimated imprecisely, we create 95 percent confidence intervals around our welfare estimates using a clustered bootstrap sampling procedure, where clusters are defined by exporter-importer pairs.[20]

Table A.2 displays our results, in which we present the top and bottom 10 countries in terms of their welfare change. On average, the United States sees a welfare loss of 0.42 percent. We discuss the larger implications of our results in the main body of this report.

TABLE A.2
Welfare Changes

Country	Welfare Change	Lower Bound	Upper Bound
Netherlands	−0.56	−0.77	−0.06
USA	−0.42	−0.58	−0.04
Germany	−0.38	−0.54	−0.04
United Kingdom	−0.38	−0.53	−0.04
Iceland	−0.28	−0.39	−0.03
Denmark	−0.26	−0.36	−0.03
France	−0.23	−0.32	−0.02
Belgium	−0.21	−0.30	−0.02
Italy	−0.16	−0.22	−0.02
Hungary	−0.12	−0.17	−0.01
Niger	0.07	0.01	0.10
Israel	0.07	0.01	0.10
Cyprus	0.07	0.01	0.11
Senegal	0.07	0.01	0.11
Trinidad and Tobago	0.08	0.01	0.11
Austria	0.10	0.01	0.14
Canada	0.11	0.01	0.16
Malta	0.11	0.01	0.16
Ireland	0.12	0.01	0.16
Mexico	0.12	0.01	0.17

NOTE: Welfare changes are calculated as the change in national expenditures relative to the change in national prices in country *i*. The Lower Bound and Upper Bound columns provide the 95% confidence interval.

---

[20] We use 2,000 replications for each scenario to create the confidence intervals around the average welfare change and real wage change.

Abbreviations

BIT	bilateral investment treaty
FDI	foreign direct investment
GDP	gross domestic product
NAFTA	North American Free Trade Agreement
NATO	North Atlantic Treaty Organization
PPML	Pseudo-Poisson Maximum Likelihood
WTO	World Trade Organization

References

Abadie, Alberto, and Javier Gardeazabal, "The Economic Costs of Conflict: A Case Study of the Basque Country," *American Economic Review*, Vol. 93, No. 1, 2003, pp. 113–132.

Allen, Michael A., Michael E. Flynn, Carla Martinez Machain, and Andrew Stravers, "Outside the Wire: U.S. Military Deployments and Public Opinion in Host States," *American Political Science Review*, Vol. 114, No. 2, 2020, pp. 326–341.

Alvarez, Fernando, and Robert E. Lucas, Jr., "General Equilibrium Analysis of the Eaton–Kortum Model of International Trade," *Journal of Monetary Economics*, Vol. 54, No. 6, 2007, pp. 1726–1768.

Anderson, James E., and Eric van Wincoop, "Trade Costs," *Journal of Economic Literature*, Vol. 42, No. 3, September 1, 2004, pp. 691–751. As of February 10, 2022: https://www.aeaweb.org/articles?id=10.1257/0022051042177649

Anderson, James E., and Yoto V. Yotov, "Terms of Trade and Global Efficiency Effects of Free Trade Agreements, 1990–2002," *Journal of International Economics*, Vol. 99, 2016, pp. 279–298.

Antràs, Pol, and Stephen R. Yeaple, "Multinational Firms and the Structure of International Trade," in Gita Gopinath, Elhanan Helpman, and Kenneth Rogoff, eds., *Handbook of International Economics*, Vol. 4, New York: Elsevier, 2014, pp. 55–130.

Arkolakis, Costas, Arnaud Costinot, and Andrés Rodríguez-Clare, "New Trade Models, Same Old Gains?" *American Economic Review*, Vol. 102, No. 1, 2012, pp. 94–130. As of February 10, 2022: https://www.aeaweb.org/articles?id=10.1257/aer.102.1.94

Art, Robert J., "A Defensible Defense: America's Grand Strategy After the Cold War," *International Security*, Vol. 15, No. 4, Spring 1991, pp. 5–53.

Azam, Jean-Paul, and Véronique Thelen, "Foreign Aid Versus Military Intervention in the War on Terror," *Journal of Conflict Resolution*, Vol. 54, No. 2, 2010, pp. 237–261.

Bagozzi, Benjamin E., and Steven T. Landis, "The Stabilizing Effects of International Politics on Bilateral Trade Flows," *Foreign Policy Analysis*, Vol. 11, No. 2, April 2015, pp. 151–171.

Baier, Scott L., Yoto V. Yotov, and Thomas Zylkin, "On the Widely Differing Effects of Free Trade Agreements: Lessons from Twenty Years of Trade Integration," *Journal of International Economics*, Vol. 116, January 1, 2019, pp. 206–226. As of February 10, 2022: https://www.sciencedirect.com/science/article/pii/S0022199618304367

Bailey, Michael A., Anton Strezhnev, and Erik Voeten, "Estimating Dynamic State Preferences from United Nations Voting Data," *Journal of Conflict Resolution*, Vol. 61, No. 2, 2017, pp. 430–456.

Bak, Daehee, "Alliance Proximity and Effectiveness of Extended Deterrence," *International Interactions*, Vol. 44, No. 1, May 2017, pp. 107–131.

Baker, Scott R., Nicholas Bloom, and Steven J. Davis, "Measuring Economic Policy Uncertainty," *Quarterly Journal of Economics*, Vol. 131, No. 4, November 2016, pp. 1593–1636.

Barry, Colin M., "Peace and Conflict at Different Stages of the FDI Lifecycle," *Review of International Political Economy*, Vol. 25, No. 2, 2018, pp. 270–292.

Beckley, Michael, "China's Century? Why America's Edge Will Endure," *International Security*, Vol. 36, No. 3, 2012, pp. 41–78.

Benson, Brett V., "Unpacking Alliances: Deterrent and Compellent Alliances and Their Relationship with Conflict, 1816–2000," *Journal of Politics*, Vol. 73, No. 4, October 2011, pp. 1111–1127.

Berger, Daniel, William Easterly, Nathan Nunn, and Shanker Satyanath, "Commercial Imperialism? Political Influence and Trade During the Cold War," *American Economic Review*, Vol. 103, No. 2, 2013, pp. 863–896.

Bhattarai, Abha, Tony Romm, and Rachel Siegel, "U.S. Economy Appeared Ready to Surge, but Russia's Invasion of Ukraine Could Send Shockwaves," *Washington Post*, February 25, 2022.

Biden, Joseph R., Jr., "Why America Must Lead Again: Recusing U.S. Foreign Policy After Trump," *Foreign Affairs*, Vol. 99, 2020, p. 64.

Biden, Joseph R., Jr., "Remarks by President Biden on America's Place in the World," White House, February 4, 2021. As of February 10, 2022:
https://www.whitehouse.gov/briefing-room/speeches-remarks/2021/02/04/remarks-by-president-biden-on-americas-place-in-the-world/

Biglaiser, Glen, and Karl DeRouen, Jr., "Following the Flag: Troop Deployment and U.S. Foreign Direct Investment," *International Studies Quarterly*, Vol. 51, No. 4, 2007, pp. 835–854.

Biglaiser, Glen, and Karl DeRouen, Jr., "The Interdependence of U.S. Troop Deployments and Trade in the Developing World," *Foreign Policy Analysis*, Vol. 5, No. 3, 2009, pp. 247–263.

Bove, Vincenzo, Leandro Elia, and Petros G. Sekeris, "U.S. Security Strategy and the Gains from Bilateral Trade," *Review of International Economics*, Vol. 22, No. 5, 2014, pp. 863–885.

Braithwaite, Alex, and Jeffrey Kucik, "Does the Presence of Foreign Troops Affect Stability in the Host Country?" *Foreign Policy Analysis*, Vol. 14, No. 4, 2018, pp. 536–560.

Brands, Hal, "Fools Rush Out? The Flawed Logic of Offshore Balancing," *Washington Quarterly*, Vol. 38, No. 2, 2015, pp. 7–28.

Brands, Hal, "U.S. Grand Strategy in an Age of Nationalism: Fortress America and Its Alternatives," *Washington Quarterly*, Vol. 40, No. 1, April 2017, pp. 73–94.

Brands, Hal, and Peter D. Feaver, "What Are America's Alliances Good For?" *Parameters*, Vol. 47, No. 2, Summer 2017, pp. 15–30. As of July 11, 2022:
https://press.armywarcollege.edu/cgi/viewcontent.cgi?article=2928&context=parameters

Brooks, Stephen G., G. John Ikenberry, and William C. Wohlforth, "Don't Come Home, America: The Case Against Retrenchment," *International Security*, Vol. 37, No. 3, 2013, pp. 7–51.

Brooks, Stephen G., and William C. Wohlforth, *World Out of Balance: International Relations and the Challenge of American Primacy*, Princeton, N.J.: Princeton University Press, 2008.

Brooks, Stephen G., and William C. Wohlforth, *America Abroad: The United States' Global Role in the 21st Century*, New York: Oxford University Press, 2016.

Bureau of Economic Analysis, "Direct Investment by Country and Industry," webpage, July 22, 2021. As of February 10, 2022:
https://www.bea.gov/data/intl-trade-investment/direct-investment-country-and-industry

Busse, Matthias, and Carsten Hefeker, "Political Risk, Institutions and Foreign Direct Investment," *European Journal of Political Economy*, Vol. 23, No. 2, 2007, pp. 397–415.

Bussmann, Margit, "Foreign Direct Investment and Militarized International Conflict," *Journal of Peace Research*, Vol. 47, No. 2, 2010, pp. 143–153.

Caliendo, Lorenzo, Maximiliano Dvorkin, and Fernando Parro, *The Impact of Trade on Labor Market Dynamics*, Cambridge, Mass., National Bureau of Economic Research, WR-21149, May 1, 2015. As of February 10, 2022:
https://www.nber.org/papers/w21149

Caliendo, Lorenzo, and Fernando Parro, "Estimates of the Trade and Welfare Effects of NAFTA," *Review of Economic Studies*, Vol. 82, No. 1, 2015, pp. 1–44. As of February 10, 2022:
https://doi.org/10.1093/restud/rdu035

Camacho, Adriana, and Catherine Rodriguez, "Firm Exit and Armed Conflict in Colombia," *Journal of Conflict Resolution*, Vol. 57, No. 1, 2013, pp. 89–116.

Carrère, Céline, and Jaime De Melo, "Non-Tariff Measures: What Do We Know, What Might Be Done?" *Journal of Economic Integration*, Vol. 26, No. 1, 2011, pp. 169–196.

Cipollina, Maria, and Luca Salvatici, "The Trade Impact of EU Tariff Margins: An Empirical Assessment," *Social Sciences*, Vol. 8, No. 9, 2019, p. 261. As of February 10, 2022:
https://www.mdpi.com/2076-0760/8/9/261

Clare, Joe, "The Deterrent Value of Democratic Allies," *International Studies Quarterly*, Vol. 57, No. 3, 2013, pp. 545–555.

Cohen, Patricia, "Within Days, Russia's War on Ukraine Squeezes the Global Economy," *New York Times*, March 1, 2022.

Colaresi, Michael P., and William R. Thompson, "Hot Spots or Hot Hands? Serial Crisis Behavior, Escalating Risks, and Rivalry," *Journal of Politics*, Vol. 64, No. 4, November 2002, pp. 1175–1198.

Costinot, Arnaud, and Andrés Rodríguez-Clare, "Chapter 4: Trade Theory with Numbers: Quantifying the Consequences of Globalization," in Gita Gopinath, Elhanan Helpman, and Kenneth Rogoff, eds., *Handbook of International Economics*, Vol. 4, New York: Elsevier, 2014, pp. 197–261. As of February 10, 2022:
https://www.sciencedirect.com/science/article/pii/B9780444543141000045

Dai, Li, Lorraine Eden, and Paul W. Beamish, "Caught in the Crossfire: Dimensions of Vulnerability and Foreign Multinationals' Exit from War-Afflicted Countries," *Strategic Management Journal*, Vol. 38, No. 7, 2017, pp. 1478–1498.

Davis, Christina L., "Linkage Diplomacy: Economic and Security Bargaining in the Anglo-Japanese Alliance, 1902–23," *International Security*, Vol. 33, No. 3, 2009, pp. 143–179.

Davis, Julie Hirschfeld, "Trump Warns NATO Allies to Spend More on Defense, or Else," *New York Times*, July 2, 2018.

De Sousa, José, Thierry Mayer, and Soledad Zignago, "Market Access in Global and Regional Trade," *Regional Science and Urban Economics*, Vol. 42, No. 6, 2012, pp. 1037–1052.

Dekel, Eddie, Matthew O. Jackson, and Asher Wollinsky, "Vote Buying: General Elections," *Journal of Political Economy*, Vol. 116, No. 2, 2008, pp. 351–380. As of February 10, 2022:
https://www.journals.uchicago.edu/doi/full/10.1086/587624?casa_token=luSon9Jw3vsAAAAA:CkbIUF4pa7OfR9jsFli4WHXs7zvW4AacaldGtiXF9EGwSpTNY5Qo2Sb34OuR-qKNaizV9VdGDjzVdg

Dekle, Robert, Jonathan Eaton, and Samuel Kortum, "Unbalanced Trade," *American Economic Review*, Vol. 97, No. 2, 2007, pp. 351–355.

Drezner, Daniel W., "Military Primacy Doesn't Pay (Nearly as Much as You Think)," *International Security*, Vol. 38, No. 1, 2013, pp. 52–79.

Drezner, Daniel W., and Nancy F. Hite-Rubin, "Does American Military Power Attract Foreign Investment?" in Jeremi Suri and Benjamin Valentino, eds., *Sustainable Security: Rethinking American National Security Strategy*, Cambridge, Mass.: The Tobin Project, 2016.

Eaton, Jonathan, and Samuel Kortum, "Technology, Geography, and Trade," *Econometrica*, Vol. 70, No. 5, 2002, pp. 1741–1779. As of February 10, 2022:
https://onlinelibrary.wiley.com/doi/pdf/10.1111/1468-0262.00352?casa_token=48U0CDWXJwM
AAAAA:3P0nBWhwVfMmmNTWFqg_qWZT51mk_ROkLOgkpGwkYVqHceXxJcWIjuYWvF
-jIdAg8qhjLCwhU6-8RizENA

Egan, Matt, "Why the Russian Invasion Will Have Huge Economic Consequences for American Families," *CNN*, February 24, 2022. As of March 7, 2022:
https://www.cnn.com/2022/02/16/economy/russia-ukraine-economy-inflation

Egel, Daniel, Adam R. Grissom, John P. Godges, Jennifer Kavanagh, and Howard J. Shatz, *Estimating the Value of Overseas Security Commitments*, Santa Monica, Calif.: RAND Corporation, RR-518-AF, 2016. As of November 23, 2020:
https://www.rand.org/pubs/research_reports/RR518.html

Egger, Peter, and Michael Pfaffermayr, "The Impact of Bilateral Investment Treaties on Foreign Direct Investment," *Journal of Comparative Economics*, Vol. 32, No. 4, 2004, pp. 788–804.

Eichengreen, Barry, Arnaud Mehl, and Livia Chiţu, "Mars or Mercury Redux: The Geopolitics of Bilateral Trade Agreements," *World Economy*, Vol. 44, No. 1, 2021, pp. 21–44.

Elkins, Zachary, Andrew T. Guzman, and Beth A. Simmons, "Competing for Capital: The Diffusion of Bilateral Investment Treaties, 1960–2000," *International Organization*, Vol. 60, No. 4, 2006, pp. 811–846.

Erickson, Jennifer L, "Saint or Sinner? Human Rights and U.S. Support for the Arms Trade Treaty," *Political Science Quarterly*, Vol. 130, No. 3, 2015, pp. 449–474.

Fang, Songying, Jesse C. Johnson, and Brett Ashley Leeds, "To Concede or to Resist? The Restraining Effect of Military Alliances," *International Organization*, Vol. 68, No. 4, 2014, pp. 775–809.

Feenstra, Robert C., Philip Luck, Maurice Obstfeld, and Katheryn N. Russ, "In Search of the Armington Elasticity," *Review of Economics and Statistics*, Vol. 100, No. 1, 2018, pp. 135–150. As of February 10, 2022:
https://doi.org/10.1162/REST_a_00696

Feldman, Nizan, and Tal Sadeh, "War and Third-Party Trade," *Journal of Conflict Resolution*, Vol. 62, No. 1, 2018, pp. 119–142.

Fordham, Benjamin O., "Trade and Asymmetric Alliances," *Journal of Peace Research*, Vol. 47, No. 6, 2010, pp. 685–696.

Frederick, Bryan, Stephen Watts, Abby Doll, Ashley L. Rhoades, and Meagan L. Smith, *Understanding the Deterrent Impact of U.S. Overseas Forces*, Santa Monica, Calif.: RAND Corporation, RR-2533-A, 2020. As of July 5, 2022:
https://www.rand.org/pubs/research_reports/RR2533.html

Freedman, David A., and Richard A. Berk, "Weighting Regressions by Propensity Scores," *Evaluation Review*, Vol. 32, No. 4, 2008, pp. 392–409.

Friedman, Benjamin H., Brendan Rittenhouse Green, Justin Logan, Stephen G. Brooks, G. John Ikenberry, and William C. Wohlforth, "Debating American Engagement: The Future of U.S. Grand Strategy," *International Security*, Vol. 38, No. 2, Fall 2013, pp. 181–199.

Friedman, Uri, "The Sanders Doctrine," *The Atlantic*, February 11, 2020. As of November 2, 2020:
https://www.theatlantic.com/politics/archive/2020/02/bernie-sanders-doctrine-america-military
-foreign-policy/606364/

Fuhrmann, Matthew, and Todd S. Sechser, "Signaling Alliance Commitments: Hand-Tying and Sunk Costs in Extended Nuclear Deterrence," *American Journal of Political Science*, Vol. 58, No. 4, 2014, pp. 919–935.

Gholz, Eugene, and Daryl G. Press, "The Effects of Wars on Neutral Countries: Why It Doesn't Pay to Preserve the Peace," *Security Studies*, Vol. 10, No. 4, 2001, pp. 1–57.

Gholz, Eugene, Daryl G. Press, and Harvey M. Sapolsky, "Come Home, America: The Strategy of Restraint in the Face of Temptation," *International Security*, Vol. 21, No. 4, 1997, pp. 5–48.

Gibler, Douglas M., *International Military Alliances, 1648–2008*, Washington, D.C.: CQ Press, 2008.

Glick, Reuven, and Alan M. Taylor, "Collateral Damage: Trade Disruption and the Economic Impact of War," *Review of Economics and Statistics*, Vol. 92, No. 1, February 2010, pp. 102–127.

Gowa, Joanne, and Raymond Hicks, "Commerce and Conflict: New Data About the Great War," *British Journal of Political Science*, Vol. 47, No. 3, 2017, pp. 653–674.

Gowa, Joanne, and Edward D. Mansfield, "Power Politics and International Trade," *American Political Science Review*, Vol. 87, No. 2, 1993, pp. 408–420.

Gowa, Joanne, and Edward D. Mansfield, "Alliances, Imperfect Markets, and Major-Power Trade," *International Organization*, Vol. 58, No. 4, 2004, pp. 775–805.

Haftel, Yoram Z., and Alexander Thompson, "Delayed Ratification: The Domestic Fate of Bilateral Investment Treaties," *International Organization*, Vol. 67, No. 2, April 2013, pp. 355–387.

Haim, Dotan A., "Alliance Networks and Trade: The Effect of Indirect Political Alliances on Bilateral Trade Flows," *Journal of Peace Research*, Vol. 53, No. 3, 2016, pp. 472–490.

Heid, Benedikt, Mario Larch, and Yoto V. Yotov, "Estimating the Effects of Non-Discriminatory Trade Policies Within Structural Gravity Models," *Canadian Journal of Economics/Revue canadienne d'économique*, Vol. 21, 2021, pp. 376–409.

Heo, Uk, and Min Ye, "U.S. Military Deployment and Host-Nation Economic Growth," *Armed Forces & Society*, Vol. 45, No. 2, 2019, pp. 234–267.

Herzer, Dierk, "Outward FDI and Economic Growth," *Journal of Economic Studies*, Vol. 37, No. 5, September 2010, pp. 476–494. As of July 22, 2022:
https://ideas.repec.org/a/eme/jespps/v37y2010i5p476-494.html

Hummels, David, "Transportation Costs and International Trade in the Second Era of Globalization," *Journal of Economic Perspectives*, Vol. 21, No. 3, Summer 2007, pp. 131–154. As of February 10, 2022:
https://www.aeaweb.org/articles?id=10.1257/jep.21.3.131

Imbs, Jean, and Isabelle Mejean, "Trade Elasticities," *Review of International Economics*, Vol. 25, No. 2, 2017, pp. 383–402. As of February 10, 2022:
https://onlinelibrary.wiley.com/doi/pdf/10.1111/roie.12270?casa_token=BEnib6ssZY4AAAAA
:10H1aCSNJ6BrYawykp7H8DHHpvUdEiOYRJMhzkbU93vIY6Z6mjiix6RAE1p-obbuyKg3jKO2
TIiQHB4gCg

Jackson, Matthew O., and Stephen Nei, "Networks of Military Alliances, Wars, and International Trade," *Proceedings of the National Academy of Sciences*, Vol. 112, No. 50, 2015, pp. 15277–15284.

Johnson, Jesse C., "The Cost of Security: Foreign Policy Concessions and Military Alliances," *Journal of Peace Research*, Vol. 52, No. 5, 2015, pp. 665–679.

Johnson, Jesse C., and Brett Ashley Leeds, "Defense Pacts: A Prescription for Peace?" *Foreign Policy Analysis*, Vol. 7, No. 1, 2011, pp. 45–65.

Johnson, Jesse C., Brett Ashley Leeds, and Ahra Wu, "Capability, Credibility, and Extended General Deterrence," *International Interactions*, Vol. 41, No. 2, 2015, pp. 309–336.

Jones, Garett, and Tim Kane, "U.S. Troops and Foreign Economic Growth," *Defence and Peace Economics*, Vol. 23, No. 3, 2012, pp. 225–249.

Kagan, Robert, "Superpowers Don't Get to Retire," *New Republic*, May 26, 2014.

Kane, Tim, "Development and U.S. Troop Deployments," *Foreign Policy Analysis*, Vol. 8, No. 3, 2012, pp. 255–273.

Kavanagh, Jennifer, *U.S. Security-Related Agreements in Force Since 1955: Introducing a New Database*, Santa Monica, Calif.: RAND Corporation, RR-736-AF, 2014. As of July 5, 2022: https://www.rand.org/pubs/research_reports/RR736.html

Kee, Hiau Looi, Alessandro Nicita, and Marcelo Olarreaga, "Estimating Trade Restrictiveness Indices," *Economic Journal*, Vol. 119, January 1, 2009, pp. 172–199. As of February 10, 2022: https://onlinelibrary.wiley.com/doi/pdf/10.1111/j.1468-0297.2008.02209.x?casa_token=TvHwP7 PmVjIAAAAA:cjWMWq9UjjkN1SZ7R89ARAWot4yYwth7KnonuRq5DC-WwoG-_b-hfE9fFcy_ -Cg1LW6uw-qXPkL7GhG5CQ

Kenwick, Michael R., John A. Vasquez, and Matthew A. Powers, "Do Alliances Really Deter?" *Journal of Politics*, Vol. 77, No. 4, 2015, pp. 943–954.

Keohane, Robert O., *After Hegemony: Cooperation and Discord in the World Political Economy*, Princeton, N.J.: Princeton University Press, 2005.

Kim, Tongfi, *The Supply Side of Security: A Market Theory of Military Alliances*, Stanford, Calif.: Stanford University Press, 2016.

Koubi, Vally, "War and Economic Performance," *Journal of Peace Research*, Vol. 42, No. 1, 2005, pp. 67–82.

Layne, Christopher, *The Peace of Illusions: American Grand Strategy from 1940 to the Present*, Ithaca, N.Y.: Cornell University Press, 2007.

Lee, Barbara, "Reps. Barbara Lee and Mark Pocan Statement on House Vote for 10% Cut to Pentagon Budget," press release, Washington, D.C., July 21, 2020. As of December 3, 2020: https://lee.house.gov/news/press-releases/reps-barbara-lee-and-mark-pocan-statement-on-house -vote-for-10-cut-to-pentagon-budget

Leeds, Brett Ashley, "Do Alliances Deter Aggression? The Influence of Military Alliances on the Initiation of Militarized Interstate Disputes," *American Journal of Political Science*, Vol. 47, No. 3, 2003, pp. 427–439.

Leeds, Brett Ashley, and Jesse C. Johnson, "Theory, Data, and Deterrence: A Response to Kenwick, Vasquez, and Powers," *Journal of Politics*, Vol. 79, No. 1, 2017, pp. 335–340.

Levine, Ross, and Sara Zervos, "Stock Market Development and Long-Run Growth," *World Bank Economic Review*, Vol. 10, No. 2, May 1996, pp. 323–339.

Li, Quan, and Tatiana Vashchilko, "Dyadic Military Conflict, Security Alliances, and Bilateral FDI Flows," *Journal of International Business Studies*, Vol. 41, No. 5, 2010, pp. 765–782.

Lichtenberg, Frank R., "Estimation of the Internal Adjustment Costs Model Using Longitudinal Establishment Data," *Review of Economics and Statistics*, Vol. 70, No. 3, 1988, pp. 421–430.

Long, Andrew G., "Defense Pacts and International Trade," *Journal of Peace Research*, Vol. 40, No. 5, 2003, pp. 537–552.

Long, Andrew G., "Bilateral Trade in the Shadow of Armed Conflict," *International Studies Quarterly*, Vol. 52, No. 1, 2008, pp. 81–101.

Long, Andrew G., and Brett Ashley Leeds, "Trading for Security: Military Alliances and Economic Agreements," *Journal of Peace Research*, Vol. 43, No. 4, 2006, pp. 433–451.

Lostumbo, Michael, Michael J. McNerney, Eric Peltz, Derek Eaton, David R. Frelinger, Victoria A. Greenfield, John Halliday, Patrick Mills, Bruce R. Nardulli, Stacie L. Pettyjohn, Jerry M. Sollinger, and Stephen M. Worman, *Overseas Basing of U.S. Military Forces: An Assessment of Relative Costs and Strategic Benefits*, Santa Monica, Calif.: RAND Corporation, RR-201-OSD, 2013. As of June 22, 2022:
https://www.rand.org/pubs/research_reports/RR201.html

Mansfield, Edward D., and Rachel Bronson, "Alliances, Preferential Trading Arrangements, and International Trade," *American Political Science Review*, Vol. 91, No. 1, 1997, pp. 94–107.

Marano, Valentina, Alvaro Cuervo-Cazurra, and Chuck C.Y. Kwok, "The Impact of Conflict Types and Location on Trade," *International Trade Journal*, Vol. 27, No. 3, June 2013, pp. 197–224.

Martin, Philippe, Thierry Mayer, and Mathias Thoenig, "Make Trade, Not War?" *Review of Economic Studies*, Vol. 75, No. 3, July 2008, pp. 865–900.

Martin, Philippe, Thierry Mayer, and Mathias Thoenig, "The Geography of Conflicts and Regional Trade Agreements," *American Economic Journal: Macroeconomics*, Vol. 4, No. 4, 2012, pp. 1–35.

Martinez Machain, Carla, and T. Clifton Morgan, "The Effect of U.S. Troop Deployment on Host States' Foreign Policy," *Armed Forces & Society*, Vol. 39, No. 1, January 2013, pp. 102–123.

Mastanduno, Michael, "System Maker and Privilege Taker: U.S. Power and the International Political Economy," *World Politics*, Vol. 61, No. 1, 2009, pp. 121–154.

Maurer, Mark, "U.S. Companies Say They Are Monitoring Impact of Russia-Ukraine Crisis," *Wall Street Journal*, February 24, 2022.

McNerney, Michael J., Angela O'Mahony, Thomas S. Szayna, Derek Eaton, Caroline Baxter, Colin P. Clarke, Emma Cutrufello, Michael McGee, Heather Peterson, Leslie A. Payne, and Calin Trenkov-Wermuth, *Assessing Security Cooperation as a Preventive Tool*, Santa Monica, Calif.: RAND Corporation, RR-350-A, 2014. As of June 22, 2022:
https://www.rand.org/pubs/research_reports/RR350.html

Mearsheimer, John J., "Why the Ukraine Crisis Is the West's Fault: The Liberal Delusions That Provoked Putin," *Foreign Affairs*, Vol. 93, 2014, p. 77.

Melitz, Marc J., "The Impact of Trade on Intra-Industry Reallocations and Aggregate Industry Productivity," *Econometrica*, Vol. 71, No. 6, 2003, pp. 1695–1725. As of February 10, 2022:
https://onlinelibrary.wiley.com/doi/abs/10.1111/1468-0262.00467?casa_token=Y3wtG6ump
4EAAAAA:EJXhLYSIX7OhyLZiwkIh2WOYnsOul4YpYnxSs8lg3qvGtVNjwY4nxZTThRN5y
QgvZ6mbYcKG2vtpSAjYCQ

Mills, Patrick, Adam R. Grissom, Jennifer Kavanagh, Leila Mahnad, and Stephen M. Worman, *A Cost Analysis of the U.S. Air Force Overseas Posture: Informing Strategic Choices*, Santa Monica, Calif.: RAND Corporation, RR-150-AF, 2013. As of January 24, 2022:
https://www.rand.org/pubs/research_reports/RR150.html

Morrow, James D., "When Do Defensive Alliances Provoke Rather Than Deter?" *Journal of Politics*, Vol. 79, No. 1, 2017, pp. 341–345.

Morrow, James D., Randolph M. Siverson, and Tressa E. Tabares, "The Political Determinants of International Trade: The Major Powers, 1907–90," *American Political Science Review*, Vol. 92, No. 3, September 1998, pp. 649–661.

Neumayer, Eric, and Laura Spess, "Do Bilateral Investment Treaties Increase Foreign Direct Investment to Developing Countries?" *World Development*, Vol. 33, No. 10, 2005, pp. 1567–1585.

Norrlof, Carla, *America's Global Advantage: U.S. Hegemony and International Cooperation*, New York: Cambridge University Press, 2010.

Nye, Joseph S., Jr. "The Changing Nature of World Power," *Political Science Quarterly*, Vol. 105, No. 2, Summer 1990, pp. 177–192.

O'Mahony, Angela, Miranda Priebe, Bryan Frederick, Jennifer Kavanagh, Matthew Lane, Trevor Johnston, Thomas S. Szayna, Jakub P. Hlavka, Stephen Watts, and Matthew Povlock, *U.S. Presence and the Incidence of Conflict*, Santa Monica, Calif.: RAND Corporation, RR-1906-A, 2018. As of July 5, 2022:
https://www.rand.org/pubs/research_reports/RR1906.html

Organski, Abramo F. K., and Jacek Kugler, "The Costs of Major Wars: The Phoenix Factor," *American Political Science Review*, Vol. 71, No. 4, 1977, pp. 1347–1366.

Pahre, Robert, *Politics and Trade Cooperation in the Nineteenth Century*, New York: Cambridge University Press, 2008.

Paul, Christopher, Michael Nixon, Heather Peterson, Beth Grill, and Jessica Yeats, *The RAND Security Cooperation Prioritization and Propensity Matching Tool*, Santa Monica, Calif.: RAND Corporation, TL-112-OSD, 2013. As of July 5, 2022:
https://www.rand.org/pubs/tools/TL112.html

Poast, Paul, "Does Issue Linkage Work? Evidence from European Alliance Negotiations, 1860 to 1945," *International Organization*, Vol. 66, Spring 2012, pp. 277–310.

Polachek, Solomon W., and Daria Sevastianova, "Does Conflict Disrupt Growth? Evidence of the Relationship Between Political Instability and National Economic Performance," *Journal of International Trade and Economic Development*, Vol. 21, No. 3, June 2012, pp. 361–388.

Posen, Barry R., *Restraint: A New Foundation for U.S. Grand Strategy*, Ithaca, N.Y.: Cornell University Press, 2014.

Pressman, Jeremy, *Warring Friends: Alliance Restraint in International Politics*, Ithaca, N.Y.: Cornell University Press, 2011.

Priebe, Miranda, Bryan Rooney, Caitlin McCulloch, and Zachary Burdette, *Do Alliances and Partnerships Entangle the United States in Conflict?* Santa Monica, Calif.: RAND Corporation, RR-A739-3, 2021. As of November 23, 2021:
https://www.rand.org/pubs/research_reports/RRA739-3.html

Qureshi, Mahvash Saeed, "Trade and Thy Neighbor's War," *Journal of Development Economics*, Vol. 105, 2013, pp. 178–195.

Rapp-Hooper, Mira, *Shields of the Republic: The Triumph and Peril of America's Alliances*, Cambridge, Mass.: Harvard University Press, 2020.

Rooney, Bryan, Grant Johnson, and Miranda Priebe, *How Does Defense Spending Affect Economic Growth?* Santa Monica, Calif.: RAND Corporation, RR-A739-2, 2021. As of January 24, 2022:
https://www.rand.org/pubs/research_reports/RRA739-2.html

Sadeh, Tal, and Nizan Feldman, "Globalization and Wartime Trade," *Cooperation and Conflict*, Vol. 55, No. 2, January 6, 2020, pp. 235–260.

Samuelson, Paul A., "The Transfer Problem and Transport Costs, II: Analysis of Effects of Trade Impediments," *Economic Journal*, Vol. 64, No. 254, 1954, pp. 264–289.

Santos Silva, Joao, and Silvana Tenreyro, "FLEX: Stata Module for Flexible Pseudo Maximum Likelihood Estimation of Models for Doubly-Bounded Data," *Economic Papers*, 2016. https://econpapers.repec.org/software/bocbocode/s457735.htm

Senese, Paul D., and John A. Vasquez, *The Steps to War: An Empirical Study*, Princeton, N.J.: Princeton University Press, 2008.

Simonovska, Ina, and Michael E. Waugh, "The Elasticity of Trade: Estimates and Evidence," *Journal of International Economics*, Vol. 92, No. 1, January 1, 2014, pp. 34–50. As of February 10, 2022: https://www.sciencedirect.com/science/article/pii/S0022199613000986

Singh, Tarlok, "Does International Trade Cause Economic Growth? A Survey," *World Economy*, Vol. 33, No. 11, November 2010, pp. 1517–1564.

Smialek, Jeanna, and Ana Swanson, "What Does Russia's Invasion of Ukraine Mean for the U.S. Economy?" *New York Times*, February 23, 2022.

Sohn, Yul, and Min Gyo Koo, "Securitizing Trade: The Case of the Korea-U.S. Free Trade Agreement," *International Relations of the Asia-Pacific*, Vol. 11, No. 3, 2011, pp. 450–454.

Stein, Arthur A., "The Hegemon's Dilemma: Great Britain, the United States, and the International Economic Order," *International Organization*, Vol. 38, No. 2, 1984, pp. 355–386.

Steinberg, Joseph B., "The Macroeconomic Impact of NAFTA Termination," *Canadian Journal of Economics/Revue canadienne d'économique*, Vol. 53, No. 2, 2020, pp. 821–865.

Stokes, Doug, and Kit Waterman, "Security Leverage, Structural Power and U.S. Strategy in East Asia," *International Affairs*, Vol. 93, No. 5, 2017, pp. 1039–1060.

Swanson, Ana, "Ukrainian Invasion Adds to Chaos for Global Supply Chains," *New York Times*, March 1, 2022.

U.S. Census, *U.S. International Trade in Goods and Services*, May 4, 2022.

U.S. Department of State, "U.S. Collective Defense Arrangements," 2017. https://2009-2017.state.gov/s/l/treaty/collectivedefense/index.htm

Villareal, M. Angeles, and Ian F. Fergusson, *NAFTA at 20: Overview and Trade Effects*, Congressional Research Service, 2014. As of July 11, 2022: https://ecommons.cornell.edu/bitstream/handle/1813/78582/CRS_Nafta_at_20_0413.pdf?sequence=1

Wadhams, Nick, and Jennifer Jacobs, "Trump Seeks Huge Premium from Allies Hosting U.S. Troops," *Bloomberg*, March 8, 2019.

Wang, Zhiyuan, and Hyunjin Youn, "Locating the External Source of Enforceability: Alliances, Bilateral Investment Treaties, and Foreign Direct Investment," *Social Science Quarterly*, Vol. 99, No. 1, May 10, 2017, pp. 80–96.

Watts, Stephen, Bryan Rooney, Gene Germanovich, Bruce McClintock, Stephanie Pezard, Clint Reach, and Melissa Shostak, *Deterrence and Escalation in Competition with Russia: Executive Summary*, Santa Monica, Calif.: RAND Corporation, RR-A720-2, 2022. As of January 24, 2022: https://www.rand.org/pubs/research_reports/RRA720-2.html

White House, *Interim National Security Strategic Guidance*, Washington, D.C., March 2021.

Wolford, Scott, and Moonhawk Kim, "Alliances and the High Politics of International Trade," *Political Science Research and Methods*, Vol. 5, No. 4, 2017, p. 587.

Wright, Thorin M., and Toby J. Rider, "Disputed Territory, Defensive Alliances and Conflict Initiation," *Conflict Management and Peace Science*, Vol. 31, No. 2, 2014, pp. 119–144.

Yamarik, Steven J., Noel D. Johnson, and Ryan A. Compton, "War! What Is it Good for? A Deep Determinants Analysis of the Cost of Interstate Conflict," *Peace Economics, Peace Science and Public Policy*, Vol. 16, No. 1, 2010.

Yotov, Yoto V., Roberta Piermartini, Jose-Antonio Monteiro, and Mario Larch, *An Advanced Guide to Trade Policy Analysis: The Structural Gravity Model Online Revised Version*, Geneva, Switzerland: World Trade Organization and the United Nations, 2016. As of February 10, 2022: https://unctad.org/system/files/official-document/gds2016d3_book_en.pdf

Zylkin, Thomas, "GE_GRAVITY: Stata Module to Solve a Simple General Equilibrium One Sector Armington-CES Trade Model," 2019. As of January 24, 2022: https://econpapers.repec.org/software/bocbocode/s458678.htm